Child Care Law
A summary of the
law in Scotland

D1513925

Published by
British Association for Adoption and Fostering
(BAAF)
Skyline House
200 Union Street
London SE1 0LX
www.baaf.org.uk

Charity registration 275689

© BAAF 2005

**British Library Cataloguing
in Publication Data**
A catalogue record for this book is available from the
British Library

ISBN 1 903699 74 6

Editorial project management by Miranda Davies
Designed by Andrew Haig & Associates
Cover illustration by Andrew Haig
Typeset by Avon Dataset Ltd, Bidford on Avon
Printed in Great Britain by Creative Print & Design

BAAF Adoption & Fostering is the leading UK-wide
membership organisation for all those concerned with
adoption, fostering and child care issues.

Child Care Law
A summary of the law in Scotland

Alexandra Plumtree

Contents

Preface

This booklet is the fifth and further revised edition of BAAF's existing title, *Child Care Law: A summary of the law in Scotland*. It takes account of the changes since the previous edition (1997), particularly the provisions of the Scotland Act 1998; of the Regulation of Care (Scotland) Act 2001 and the creation of the Care Commission; of the Adoption (Intercountry Aspects) Act 1999 and its supporting regulations and court rules; and of the effects in Scotland of the Adoption and Children Act 2002.

As with previous editions, this book is not a detailed legal textbook about what is a wide-reaching area of law. Rather, it aims to provide a basic framework of the law for those who do not need to know more **and** a starting point for those who have to look further. Statutory references[1] are given throughout the text with abbreviations listed in Chapter 1. There is a glossary of terms and a list of further reading and useful websites.

I should like to thank all of those who have given and continue to give me the benefit of their views on the many issues of law and practice that are continuously arising in this area of law. In particular, I am grateful to Janys Scott, Advocate, for reading the text and providing detailed comments and corrections. Any mistakes remaining are, of course, mine. I am also grateful to all my colleagues in BAAF Scotland for their help and support, and to Miranda Davies and Shaila Shah in our Publications Department in London.

I have tried to state the law as at **30 September 2005**.

Alexandra Plumtree
Solicitor and Legal Consultant, BAAF Scotland

---

[1] Where statutory references are given at the end of a paragraph, section, rule and regulation numbers are listed in the order they are covered in that paragraph, not in numerical order.

Note about the author

Alexandra Plumtree is a solicitor and the Legal Consultant with BAAF Scotland. She has worked in private practice and as a children's reporter, and has extensive experience of the public and private law for children and families in Scotland. She was the Independent Legal Adviser to the Scottish Executive's Adoption Policy Review Group from 2001 to 2005.

1 Introduction and abbreviations

This chapter sets out the main legislative background for child care law in Scotland, and other relevant provisions. It includes an outline of devolution, and gives abbreviations for legislation, etc, and other terms used in the text.

Devolution

1.1

The **Scotland Act 1998 (the 1998 Act)** established the Scottish Parliament, Holyrood, from July 1999. As a result, Acts applying in Scotland may either be passed by the Westminster Parliament or by Holyrood. Those dated before 1999 will be from Westminster, but those after then could be from either Parliament. Acts with "Scotland" (or a clear reference to Scotland) in their title apply to Scotland, but in other Acts, it is necessary to check the "Extent" section near the end, to find out which part or parts of the UK they apply to.

1.2

Holyrood can only legislate about **"devolved"** matters, not anything which is **"retained"** by Westminster. But the 1998 Act says that unless a matter listed in it is reserved to Westminster, it is devolved to Holyrood.

1.3

Most things which affect day-to-day life are devolved, such as education, social work, health services, local authorities, property law, family law, the police and criminal law. Retained matters, which Holyrood cannot usually pass laws about, include the benefits system, immigration law, employment law, defence, foreign affairs and anti-discrimination law. Holyrood cannot change the basic rules about them, but it can legislate to implement policy and practice in these areas. Conversely, Holyrood can "give back" to Westminster the power to make law on devolved matters, if Members of Scottish Parliament (MSPs) vote for this in a Sewel motion. For example, Holyrood allowed the Adoption and Children Act 2002 to include some provisions for Scotland, although most of the Act does not apply in Scotland. And the Civil Partnership Act 2004 passed by Westminster was allowed to include devolved issues as well as retained ones, so that similar provisions could be covered for the whole of the UK.

Statutory background

1.4

Many of the provisions are referred to in more detail in later chapters and references are given here. Others are relevant to the general application of the law, such as the Human Rights Act 1998.

Acts of Parliament and Conventions

1.5

European Convention on Human Rights 1950   **ECHR**
See the Human Rights Act 1998 below.

The Race Relations Act 1976, as amended by the Race Relations (Amendment) Act 2000, includes provisions obliging public authorities (including local authorities) to promote racial equality, equal opportunities and good race relations, and to eliminate unlawful discrimination in all their work, including service delivery, policy making and employment. These provisions have clear relevance to all children and family services provided by local authorities. Authorities need to be clear about how all their policies and services affect race equality.

Adoption (Scotland) Act 1978   **1978 Act**
This is the current adoption legislation in Scotland, although new legislation to replace it is planned, following the Report of the Adoption Policy

Review Group in June 2005. It replaced earlier adoption legislation going back to 1930 and incorporates amendments by the Children (Scotland) Act 1995 and the Adoption (Intercountry Aspects) Act 1999. See Chapters 13–15.

Foster Children (Scotland) Act 1984   1984 Act

This is the Act governing private fostering, along with the 1985 Regs. See Chapter 6, *Private arrangements* and Chapter 10, *Fostering*.

UN Convention on the Rights of the Child 1989

Unlike the ECHR, this has not been incorporated into UK law and remains persuasive only.

Human Fertilisation and Embryology Act 1990   HFEA 1990

This set up the Human Fertilisation and Embryology Authority and contains the law about assisted conception, including the making of "parental orders" in surrogacy cases. See Chapter 4.

Age of Legal Capacity (Scotland) Act 1991   1991 Act

This Act sets out the ages at which children and young people attain legal capacity in civil matters. See Chapter 2.

Children (Scotland) Act 1995   1995 Act

This is the principal Act for private and public law about children in Scotland. It covers:

- Private law in Part I of the Act. See Chapters 2 and 4 of this book.
- Local authority public law duties and powers in Chapter 1 of Part II of the Act. See Chapters 7, 9 and 10.
- Children's hearing system in Chapters 2 and 3 of Part II of the Act. These provisions replace those in the Social Work (Scotland) Act 1968, which established the system. See Chapter 11.
- Short-term orders for child protection in Chapter 3 of Part II of the Act. See Chapter 8.
- Parental responsibilities orders (PROs) in Chapter 4 of Part II of the Act. See Chapter 12.
- Definitions for **all** the provisions in Part II of the Act in s. 93.

In addition, Part III and Schedule 2 of the 1995 Act substantially amended the 1978 Act. However, these provisions should be read in and referred to from an up-to-date text of the 1978 Act, and not quoted from the 1995 Act.

Data Protection Act 1998   **DPA 1998**

This Act applies to the whole of the UK and governs the keeping and release of personal data held on file about individuals. This includes social work and education information held by local authorities. Individuals are entitled to access personal data held on them and this cannot be shared with others without their consent, although there are exceptions to these rules. The system is very complicated and is monitored by the UK Information Commissioner. Under the subject access provisions, individuals are entitled to seek access to their own personal data in social work files, but all adoption agency records are specifically exempt from the subject access provisions by regulations.

Human Rights Act 1998   **HRA 1998**

This Act gives effect throughout the UK to the rights and freedoms guaranteed under the 1950 ECHR. The actings of all public authorities including courts, local authorities and other agencies must be compatible with the ECHR.

Regulation of Care (Scotland) Act 2001   **2001 Act**

This established a system for regulation, registration and inspection of a wide range of care services. It also set up the Scottish Commission for the Regulation of Care – the Care Commission – and the Scottish Social Services Council. See Chapter 5.

Protection of Children (Scotland) Act 2003   **POCSA 2003**

This introduced a duty on Scottish Ministers to maintain a list of people considered unsuitable to work with children. There are duties on organisations to refer people for possible inclusion and consequences for all people who work with children, whether in employment or on a voluntary basis. See Chapter 8.

Civil Partnership Act 2004   **CPA 2004**

This will be in force throughout the UK from 5 December 2005. It allows same-sex couples to enter into formal civil partnerships and these will have considerable legal consequences in a wide range of matters, including inheritance, property, taxation and immigration. It has different provisions for the different parts of the UK. It does **not** have provisions for Scotland about parental responsibilities and rights for children, but see Chapter 4, paragraph 4.22. It does **not** enable same-sex couples to adopt in the UK. This will be possible in England and Wales from 30 December 2005 under the 2002 Act and may be introduced later in Scotland in new adoption legislation. See Chapters 13 and 14.

Antisocial Behaviour etc. (Scotland) Act 2004   **ASBA 2004**

This introduced various provisions affecting children. It is covered in Chapter 11 for convenience because many of the measures may involve the reporter and hearings, although it is not really part of that system.

Family Law (Scotland) Bill   **FL(S)B**

This Bill was introduced in February 2005 and is expected to become the FL(S) Act 2005 or 2006. It covers a range of issues, including parental responsibilities for unmarried fathers (see Chapter 4, paragraph 4.15) and increased rights for separating unmarried couples.

Regulations

1.6

Foster Children (Private Fostering) (Scotland) Regulations 1985

                                                           1985 Regs

These govern private fostering along with the 1984 Act. See Chapters 6 and 10.

Children's Hearings (Scotland) Rules 1996   **CH Rules**

These govern the organisation and running of hearings. See Chapter 11.

Arrangements to Look After Children (Scotland) Regulations 1996

LA Regs 1996

These set out the rules to be followed by local authorities for **all** looked after children, including care plans, reviews and medical assessments – see Chapter 9. There are additional rules for some groups of looked after children, such as those who are fostered (see below) and those in secure accommodation.

Fostering of Children (Scotland) Regulations 1996   F Regs 1996
These set out the rules for local authorities and voluntary agencies in the **public** fostering of looked after children. See Chapter 10.

Adoption Agencies (Scotland) Regulations 1996   Ad Ag Regs 1996
These set out the rules for local authority and voluntary adoption agencies in the running of their services (see Chapter 13), including planning for children who are to be adopted. There are also intercountry adoption regulations. See Chapter 15.

Support and Assistance of Young People Leaving Care (Scotland) Regulations 2003   Leaving Care Regs 2003
These set out detailed duties on local authorities to those young people for whom they have "aftercare" duties under s. 29 of the 1995 Act, as amended by the 2001 Act. There is also Guidance (see below). See Chapter 9, paragraph 9.11.

Court rules

1.7

Act of Sederunt (Sheriff Court Ordinary Cause Rules) 1993 (as amended)   OCR 1993
These are for a wide range of sheriff court cases called "Ordinary Causes". They include applications in family cases under the 1995 Act, such as residence and contact orders, and divorce proceedings. These rules govern the preparation of court reports, which may be ordered in these cases. See Chapter 4.

Act of Sederunt (Rules of the Court of Session) 1994 (as amended) RCS 1994

These are court rules for Court of Session cases, with Forms. They cover all cases, including *Family Actions*, Chapter 49, and *Adoption*, Chapter 67.

Act of Sederunt (Child Care and Maintenance Rules) 1997 AS 1997

These are the sheriff court rules for a range of child care and other proceedings. Chapter 2 of the rules covers adoption and freeing (Chapters 13 and 15 in this book), PROs (Chapter 12) and HFEA 1990 applications (Chapter 4). Chapter 3 of the rules covers children's hearing cases in the sheriff court (Chapter 11) and applications for CAOs, CPOs and EOs (Chapter 8).

Guidance

1.8

The Guidance on the 1995 Act is an important tool for all those working with children and families. See Further Reading for details of how to access these on the web. They are collectively called **Scotland's Children: The Children (Scotland) Act 1995, Regulations and Guidance**.

- Volume 1: *Support and Protection for Children and their Families*
- Volume 2: *Children Looked After by Local Authorities*
- Volume 3: *Adoption and Parental Responsibilities Orders*
- *Supporting Young People Leaving Care in Scotland: Regulations and Guidance on Services for Young People Ceasing to be Looked After by Local Authorities*

Standards

1.9

Under the 2001 Act, many **National Care Standards** have been produced, including:

National Care Standards: Foster Care and Family Placement Services

Fostering Standards

National Care Standards: Adoption Agencies

Adoption Standards

See Chapters 5, 6, 10, 13 and 15.

Other abbreviations

1.10

Legislation

1937 Act	Children and Young Persons (Scotland) Act 1937
1968 Act	Social Work (Scotland) Act 1968
1975 Act	Children Act 1975
1985 Act	Family Law (Scotland) Act 1985
1986 Act	Law Reform (Parent and Child) (Scotland) Act 1986
FLA 1986	Family Law Act 1986
1989 Act	Children Act 1989
CSA 1991	Child Support Act 1991
CP(S)A 1995	Criminal Procedure (Scotland) Act 1995
Ad All Regs 1996	Adoption Allowance (Scotland) Regulations 1996
1999 Act	Adoption (Intercountry Aspects) Act 1999
2002 Act	Adoption and Children Act 2002
MHA 2003	Mental Health (Care and Treatment) (Scotland) Act 2003
Regis Regs 2003	Registration of Foreign Adoptions (Scotland) Regulations 2003

Other terms

ASBO	Antisocial behaviour order – see Chapter 11
CAO	Child assessment order – see Chapter 8
CPO	Child protection order – see Chapter 8
EO	Exclusion order – see Chapter 8
PF	Procurator fiscal
PRO	Parental responsibilities order – see Chapter 12
r. or rr.	specific rule(s)
reg. or regs.	specific Regulation(s)
s. or ss.	specific section(s) of an Act

2 Principles and themes

This chapter deals with general themes and principles in the law of Scotland relating to children, some of which are in the 1995 Act.

Definition of "child"

2.1

There is no single definition of child in the law of Scotland. Whether a young person is a "child" or not will depend on the particular legislation and/or circumstances. However, as a rule of thumb, 16-year-olds in Scotland can do most things legally except vote and buy alcohol (18) or drive (17). In private disputes about children between parents and other carers, the law usually regulates the position only up to 16, although parents are obliged to pay maintenance for their children beyond that time and up to the age of 25 if in full-time education. Where a child is looked after by the local authority, that care can last up to 18 and there is provision for after-care beyond that.

Some other definitions

2.2

There is a distinction between criminal and civil law. Criminal law is self-explanatory and, for the purposes of this book, anything which is not criminal will be treated as civil.

2.3

Another distinction is made between private and public law. For the purposes of this book, private law relates to matters between private individuals and their rights and responsibilities in relation to each other. Public law deals with the ways in which society and the state become involved in the lives of children and families. Adoption law straddles this divide, as it is a private law action in the courts, but often (not always) comes about because of public law intervention by the local authority.

Principles to be applied

2.4

The 1995 Act sets out principles which apply to most decisions in the areas of the law that the Act deals with. Those areas are private law, local authority duties, child protection measures, the children's hearing system, PROs and adoption. These principles are set out below.

Child's welfare to be paramount consideration

2.5

This was not a completely new test in all types of cases in the 1995 Act. However, it is the test which now applies in court decisions (except about evidence), children's hearing decisions and local authority and adoption agencies' decisions about welfare in the areas listed in paragraph 2.4 above. In private law cases this has been the test since 1986, but in adoption matters the test was previously "first consideration" of the child's welfare. In fact, the adoption test is that the child's welfare throughout the child's life shall be of paramount consideration, while in all other cases it is the child's welfare throughout childhood.

1995 Act, s.11(7)(a), s.16(1) and s.17(1)(a); 1978 Act, s.6(1)(a)

Consideration of the child's views

2.6

Parents, courts, children's hearings, local authorities and adoption agencies all have a duty to allow children to express their views about their situations, and to take account of these views in their decisions. While this had been good practice in many areas, the 1995 Act formally specifies it as a duty in these situations. There is no **lower** age limit. The 1995 Act says that children who are 12 or over are presumed to have views, and this clearly implies that younger children can have views

although they are not presumed to have them. It is necessary for courts, hearings, authorities and agencies to find out:
- if children have views,
- whether they wish to express them, and if so,
- to take account of the views.

However, this does not mean the same thing as doing exactly what children want.

1995 Act, s.6(1), s.11(7)(b) and (10), s.16(2) and (4), s.17(3) and (4) and s.25(5); 1978 Act, s.6(1)(b)(i) and (2)

Minimum necessary intervention

2.7

This principle is sometimes called the "no order" principle. It states that no court order or children's hearing requirement shall be made unless the court/hearing thinks that making an order is better for the child than not making it. This does not mean that making an order is a "last resort". It means that the court or hearing must be certain that an order is necessary for the child's welfare, and that the order it is making is the best one. If the child's welfare can be secured as paramount consideration without an order or with less of an order, that is what should be done. Adoption agencies have a similar duty when they are making any decisions relating to the adoption/freeing of a child: they must consider alternatives.

1995 Act, s.11(7)(a) and s.16(3) and (4); 1978 Act, s.6A and s.24(3)

Consideration of religious persuasion, racial, cultural and linguistic heritage

2.8

This principle was introduced by the 1995 Act but does not apply to all areas of law. It applies to decisions that the local authority make in relation to children whom they are "looking after" or whom they are treating as "in need". It is also a duty on adoption agencies and courts in any decision relating to adoption. There is no mention of it in Part I of the 1995 Act, about private law. However, there is case law indicating that these matters are important and need to be considered in private law cases.

1995 Act, s.17(4)(c) and s.22(2); 1978 Act, s.6(1)(b)(ii); Osborne v Matthan 1997 SLT 811 (18 October 1996).

Capacity of children: criminal and civil

2.9

The age of criminal capacity in Scotland is eight.

2.10

The age of civil capacity in Scotland is generally 16, but with specific exceptions. These are that a child under 16:
- may carry out normal transactions (e.g. buy sweets, trainers, etc);
- may make a will if 12 or over;
- must be asked if he or she consents to adoption if 12 or over (unless incapable);
- must be the person to consent or otherwise to medical, dental and surgical treatment if, in the opinion of the qualified medical practitioner, he or she is capable of understanding the nature and possible consequences of the treatment;
- may instruct a solicitor in any civil matter if he or she has a general understanding of what it means to do so.

The most striking of these are the rights to consent to medical treatment and to instruct a solicitor.

1991 Act, s.1 and s.2, particularly s.2(4), (4A) and (4B)

Medical consent for children

2.11

Consent to medical treatment must come from the young person under 16 **when** a medical practitioner considers her or him to be capable of understanding the nature and consequences of the treatment (see paragraph 2.10). It is considered that the right to consent includes the right to refuse to consent. Parental consent is not needed in these circumstances and cannot override the child's consent or refusal, but it is good practice to work with the family as a whole if possible. The law is different from that in England and Wales.

1991 Act, s.2(4)

Mental health

2.12

Mental health law in Scotland was contained in the Mental Health (Scotland) Act 1984. This was replaced from 5 October 2005 with the MHA 2003. Both Acts have no lower age limit and may be used for children and young people. The MHA 2003 has more provisions than the previous Act to take account of the welfare and interests of children and other patients.

MHA 2003

Working co-operatively

2.13

Good co-operative working between all individuals making decisions about children or working with them and their families is positively encouraged by the 1995 Act, in private and public law cases. There is an expectation that parents will work together and with their children in all decisions about welfare, even if the parents themselves do not get on. There is an expectation that, where the local authority is involved with children and families, they will work co-operatively and in partnership with them.

Local authority

2.14

"Local authority" is defined in the 1995 Act as meaning the whole local authority and all its departments, not just the social work department. This was a change from the position under the 1968 Act. It means that the whole local authority are obliged to carry out responsibilities, duties, etc.

when they are owed to children and families, whether the children are "in need", "looked after" or requiring other services.

1995 Act, s.93(1)

Disclosure checks

2.15

The Police Act 1997 introduced a new system for disclosing criminal history information to individuals and organisations for employment and other purposes. Disclosure Scotland is the body which arranges for checks. With the implementation of POCSA 2003 in 2005 (see Chapter 8, paragraphs 8.24 and 8.25) there are many people for whom checks must now be made.

Police Act 1997, Part V; POCSA 2003

2.16

There are three levels of Disclosure: Basic, Standard and Enhanced. Basic ones only show convictions which are not unspent in terms of the Rehabilitation of Offenders Act 1974. Standard Disclosures contain all convictions, whether spent or unspent in terms of the 1974 Act. Enhanced Disclosures contain all convictions and any "police intelligence" about the subject. These are the ones sought for people working directly with or caring for children. Anyone can apply for a Basic Disclosure for themselves. Only registered organisations may seek Standard and Enhanced Disclosures for employees, prospective carers, and others, including those working with children, whether in a paid or unpaid capacity.

3 Scottish courts and the criminal system

This chapter outlines briefly the Scottish court structure and explains some points about the Scottish criminal system in general. Different decisions are made in different courts. Who makes a decision and the procedure used depends on which court is dealing with a case.

The court system

3.1

The Scottish court system is reasonably straightforward. There are three courts which deal with civil matters:

- sheriff courts;
- Court of Session;
- House of Lords.

And there are three courts which deal with criminal matters:

- district courts;
- sheriff courts;
- High Court.

3.2

All courts are public authorities under the HRA 1998, so all court decisions must take account of the ECHR.

HRA 1998

3.3

In addition, it is possible for an appeal raising devolution issues to go to the Judicial Committee of the Privy Council, from the Court of Session or the House of Lords in civil matters; or from the High Court in criminal matters. This is a limited option under the Scotland Act 1998 and has so far been used almost only in criminal matters.

3.4

The sheriff court operates in both civil and criminal cases and deals with the widest variety of matters. Scotland is divided into six sheriffdoms and each sheriffdom has a Sheriff Principal. There are 50 sheriff court districts, each of which has a court where a sheriff sits regularly. Sheriffs are either permanent judges, or part-time ones. Both of these have to be legally qualified and have had a number of years' experience. Honorary sheriffs are appointed locally to deal with certain matters when there is a shortage of other sheriffs. They are often not legally qualified and have very limited powers.

3.5

Sheriffs Principal and sheriffs are addressed as "My Lord" or "My Lady" in court and "Sheriff Principal" or "Sheriff" when off the bench.

Civil courts

The sheriff court

3.6

The sheriff court deals with a wide variety of civil matters. Only the sheriff court can hear children's hearing proof cases, appeals from children's hearings and applications about PROs. The sheriff court deals with many cases of divorce and disputes about children and adoption, although these can also be raised in the Court of Session.

3.7

An appeal from a sheriff can go either to the Sheriff Principal for that area or straight to the Court of Session. If there is an appeal to the Sheriff Principal, there may be a further appeal on to the Court of Session. Where a case is started, and where any appeal goes, are decisions for the person raising the case and the person who appeals.

The Court of Session

3.8

This court deals with civil cases from the beginning, and also appeals in civil cases. It sits only in Edinburgh. The judges are legally qualified and are the same as those who sit in the High Court of Justiciary. They may be permanent or temporary appointments and are addressed as "My Lord" or "My Lady".

3.9

If a case is started in the Court of Session, it is heard by a single judge in the "Outer House". If the court is sitting as an appeal court, a group of three or more judges sits to hear the case in the "Inner House". They deal with appeals from sheriffs, Sheriffs Principal and the Outer House.

3.10

The senior judge in Scotland and the head of the Scottish legal system is the Lord President of the Court of Session and also the Lord Justice General in criminal cases.

House of Lords

3.11

There is an appeal in some but not all civil matters from the Inner House of the Court of Session to the House of Lords. Adoption appeals and appeals in private law disputes about children go to the House of Lords, but appeals in children's hearing cases cannot do so.

3.12

Cases are heard by an appellate (appeal) committee of the House of Lords. The judges are called Lords of Appeal in Ordinary or Law Lords. Usually five of them hear a case and if it is a Scottish appeal, two of those judges will, by convention, be Scottish. At any one time, there are always two Scottish Law Lords.

3.13

These judges sit in the House of Lords as Life Peers, the senior Law Lord being the Lord Chancellor. He is also speaker of the House of Lords, and is a political appointment. He is head of the legal system for England and Wales, but not of the Scottish legal system. There are plans to substitute a Supreme Court for the UK in place of the appellate committee of the House of Lords, and if and when this occurs, appeals from the Inner House of the Court of Session will go there instead of to the House of Lords.

The Scottish criminal system

3.14

Prosecution in Scotland is carried out by the independent prosecution service. This is headed by the Crown Office and represented locally by procurators fiscal (PF). Decisions to prosecute are made on the basis of the following questions:
- is there sufficient evidence? **and**
- is it in the public interest to prosecute?

The prosecution decides what offence a person will be charged with and which court will deal with the matter. A case is either **summary**, when it is dealt with by a judge alone; or **solemn**, when it is dealt with by a judge and jury. There is no right to jury trial in Scotland and the number of jurors is 15.

3.15

In Scotland, the adult criminal system is not used for most cases involving crimes alleged to have been committed by children under 16. Even though the age of criminal capacity is eight, most children are not prosecuted in the courts. Instead, they are referred by the police to the children's reporter, who decides whether to take the case to a children's hearing (see Chapter 11). The major exception to this rule is where a child is charged with a more serious offence, such as a severe assault or murder. In those circumstances the child will be dealt with by the adult criminal system.

3.16

By and large, the police report children under 16 only to the reporter. They may also report cases to the procurator fiscal. If a case is jointly reported, the PF makes the ultimate decision about whether the child is dealt with in the adult system even if he or she is still subject to a supervision requirement in the hearing system.

3.17

The ASBA 2004 introduced various provisions affecting young people under 16. These involve the courts in a civil and criminal capacity, and the hearing system. These are covered below, in Chapter 11, paragraphs 11.37–11.42.

ASBA 2004

Criminal courts

The district court

3.18

This court deals only with minor criminal matters. Cases are heard by one or more lay, unqualified justices, sitting with a legally qualified clerk. In Glasgow District Court, there are a number of stipendiary magistrates who are legally qualified and sit on their own. As in all criminal courts, cases come to this one on the basis of a decision by the prosecution service.

The sheriff court

3.19

Sheriff courts deal with the bulk of criminal cases in Scotland. They deal both with summary matters (lesser crimes) where a sheriff sits and hears the case on his or her own; and more serious cases, solemn matters, which are heard by a sheriff sitting with a jury. Again, the decision to take a case to the sheriff court, and whether with or without a jury, is made by the prosecution service.

The High Court of Justiciary

3.20

This is the court which deals with serious criminal trials and with **all** criminal appeals in Scotland. The judges are the same as those in the Court of Session.

3.21

If the High Court is dealing with a criminal trial, this is done by a single judge sitting with a jury. The court can try all crimes, but usually only deals with very serious ones. Only the High Court can deal with murder, treason and rape. The court goes on circuit around the country.

3.22

When the court is sitting to hear appeals, it sits only in Edinburgh. A group of two or more judges will hear criminal appeals, from the district court and the sheriff court, as well as from High Court trials. This is the final court of appeal in Scotland for criminal matters. There is no criminal appeal in Scotland to the House of Lords. However, since 1999, cases which raise devolution issues may be appealed to the Judicial Committee of the Privy Council.

4 Parentage and parental responsibilities and rights – private law

This chapter deals with parentage of children and parental responsibilities and rights in relation to them. It covers who are parents, who has responsibilities and rights, who can get them and how, together with how the court deals with disputes in this area. "Parental responsibilities and rights" are referred to as "responsibilities and rights".

Parentage: legal mother and father

4.1

The rules of parentage are about who is considered to be the legal mother or father of a child. These rules do **not** say who has responsibilities and rights for a child. That is covered below in paragraphs 4.9 onwards.

4.2

The common, non-statutory law did not deal with who was/is the legal mother of a child, because it is only recently that there was any possibility that the gestational mother could be a different person from the genetic mother. In most cases, there is no physical difference. However, the HFEA 1990 now states that the carrying, gestational mother is the legal mother, not the genetic mother if she is a different person. So when a child is born as a result of assisted conception, the gestational mother is the legal mother even if she is not the genetic mother. And when a child is born to a surrogate mother, she is the legal mother. The legal genetic mother automatically has responsibilities and rights. See below, paragraph 4.13.

HFEA 1990, s.27

4.3

In unassisted conception, the genetic father is the legal father. There may be uncertainty about who is the genetic father without DNA testing. Unlike the position of mothers, many genetic legal fathers do not have responsibilities and rights automatically. See below, paragraphs 4.14 onwards.

4.4

In unassisted conception, the 1986 Act has two presumptions about who is the legal father. A presumption is a general legal rule and may be challenged and rebutted by going to court and proving it untrue in a particular case. In cases about paternity, that is often shown by DNA evidence. The presumptions are:

- a man married to the mother at any time between the conception and the birth of a child is presumed to be the legal, genetic father. He automatically has responsibilities and rights and keeps them unless and until the presumption is rebutted;
- a man not married to the mother of a child is presumed to be the legal, genetic father **if** both he and the mother acknowledge him as the father **and** the child has been registered as his child. He does not have responsibilities and rights.

1986 Act, s.5

4.5

If there is a dispute about who is the legal father, a court can be asked to grant an order about paternity or non-paternity, called a Declarator. If a father obtains a Declarator of Paternity, this raises the presumption that he is the legal, genetic father as if his name was on the birth certificate. But it does not give him responsibilities and rights. However, if a man married to the legal mother obtains a Declarator of Non-paternity, he loses the responsibilities and rights which he had.

1986 Act, s.7

4.6

In assisted conception, the rules about who is the legal father are complex.

- If a woman conceives using her partner's sperm, he is the legal father but will only automatically have responsibilities and rights if married to the mother.
- If a women conceives using anonymous sperm and her partner consented to this, he is the legal father but will only automatically have responsibilities and rights if married to the mother.
- If a women conceives using anonymous sperm through a registered clinic and her partner did not consent to this, the child has no legal father.
- If a women conceives using sperm from a deceased donor, the child has no legal father.

As with other fathers who do not have responsibilities and rights, there are ways in which these can be obtained. See below, paragraphs 4.17–4.28.

HFEA 1990, s.28 and s.29

Surrogacy

4.7

When a child is born to a surrogate mother, she is the legal parent and has parental responsibilities and rights. If she is married and her husband agreed to the surrogacy, he is the legal father and also has responsibilities and rights. If he did not agree, he is not the legal father and has no responsibilities and rights. The genetic father is the legal father with no responsibilities and rights. If she is not married, she is the sole legal parent.

HFEA 1999, s.28

4.8

The people who commission the surrogacy are not legal parents and have no responsibilities and rights. They may acquire these with the consent of the legal parent(s) by a parental order under the HFEA 1990. If there is no consent, they may seek adoption which may be granted even if money has been paid for the surrogacy.

HFEA 1990, s.30

Parental responsibilities and rights

4.9

The 1995 Act introduced the terminology of "parental responsibilities and rights", instead of just "parental rights". Traditionally, Scots law treated children as the possession of their parents but the 1995 Act moved away from this, towards treating children as people who have their own rights as well.

4.10

Sections 1 and 2 of the 1995 Act deal with responsibilities and rights, and make it clear that rights are given to enable the carrying out of responsibilities. The responsibilities are:
• to safeguard and protect the child's welfare;
• to provide guidance;
• to maintain contact if not living with the child; and
• to act as the child's legal representative if need be.

The rights are:
• to have the child living with him or her;
• to control, direct or guide the child;
• to maintain contact if not living with the child; and
• to act as the child's legal representative if need be.

1995 Act, s.1 and s.2

4.11

These rights can be exercised individually by any person having them, without having to obtain the consent of anyone else who also has them.

The only exception is that the child cannot be removed from the United Kingdom without the consent of every person who has the responsibilities and rights of residence and/or contact **and** is exercising them.

1995 Act, s.2(2), (3) and (6)

Duty to maintain

4.12

The mother and father, whether married or not, are both obliged to maintain a child even if they do not have any responsibilities and rights, unless the child has been adopted or made the subject of an order under the HFEA 1990. This is dealt with by the 1985 Act, not the 1995 Act. Since the coming into force of the CSA 1991, when parents have separated and there is a dispute about maintenance, the Child Support Agency will usually be involved instead of the court.

1985 Act, s.1; 1978 Act, s.12; HFEA 1990, s.30; CSA 1991

Who has responsibilities and rights automatically?

4.13

The legal mother of a child always has responsibilities and rights unless and until these are taken away from her by some form of court process such as adoption or a parental order under the HFEA 1990.

1995 Act, s.3

4.14

The legal father only has responsibilities and rights automatically in Scotland at present (2005) if he has been or is married to the mother at the time of the child's conception or anytime subsequently. Where a couple are married and have children, both parents will have responsibilities and rights. If the couple are not married, the father does not have those responsibilities and rights automatically, even if he is on the birth certificate as father and/or has a Declarator of Paternity. If he marries the mother at any time after the child's birth, he acquires these. If a man marries a woman with children, but he is not the genetic, legal father, he does not acquire parental responsibilities and rights because of the marriage.

1995 Act, s.3

4.15

However, the FL(S)B introduced to the Scottish Parliament in 2005 proposes that an unmarried father who is named as father on a child's birth certificate will automatically have full responsibilities and rights. When this comes into force (possibly 2006), it will apply to any child born after that date and whose father is not married to the mother but who is shown on the birth certificate. It will not be retrospective. See Chapter 1, paragraph 1.4

FL(S)B

4.16

In England and Wales and Northern Ireland, the law was changed in 2003, so unmarried fathers on birth certificates for children born since then have automatic parental responsibility. These provisions are not retrospective. They need to be remembered when working with families who have moved to Scotland from other parts of the UK.

1989 Act, s.4 (as amended by the 2002 Act); Children (Northern Ireland) Order 1995, Article 7 (as amended)

How can unmarried fathers acquire responsibilities and rights?

4.17

An unmarried genetic father can acquire responsibilities and rights by using the agreement provided for in s. 4 of the 1995 Act. There is a straightforward form. When it is signed by both genetic parents and sent for registration in the Books of Council and Session (a public register), it gives the father full responsibilities and rights as if he had married the mother. There is a small cost for this, but no formal procedure is involved, and there is no need to go to court. Forms are available from organisations such as Citizens Advice Bureaux. However, they cannot be used by anyone who is not a genetic parent.

1995 Act, s.4

4.18

A section 4 form provides a straightforward way for a couple to give the unmarried father responsibilities and rights without going to court or being involved in a dispute. There is no need for the couple to live together. Once this agreement is signed and registered, the couple cannot change their minds. The only way to alter the arrangements after that is to go to court.

1995 Act, s.4(4)

4.19

An unmarried father can also apply to court under s. 11 of the 1995 Act (see paragraphs 4.20 onwards) to obtain responsibilities and rights. He has to do this if the mother disagrees with his request for responsibilities and rights, and refuses to sign a s.4 form. He may also want to use s. 11 if he does not want all responsibilities and rights but only, say, contact.

1995 Act, s.11

Acquiring responsibilities and rights – section 11 applications and orders

4.20

Section 11 of the 1995 Act allows courts (the sheriff court or Court of Session) to make any type of order about responsibilities and rights, guardianship or a child's property. The court may make an order because it has been asked to do so, or simply when, in any other case, it thinks an order is necessary.

1995 Act, s.11(1), (2) and (3)

4.21

The most common types of s. 11 orders are:
- residence orders;
- contact orders;
- specific issue orders;
- interdicts;
- orders giving responsibilities and rights;
- orders taking away some or all of a person's responsibilities and rights.

1995 Act, s.11(2)

4.22

Any person can use this section, provided he or she can claim an interest in the child. This includes all parents with responsibilities and rights, birth fathers without them and anyone else claiming an interest, including step-parents of children, whether married, unmarried or same-sex partners. The only individuals who cannot use the court in this way are people who have already lost their responsibilities and rights because of adoption, freeing orders or PROs.

1995 Act, s.11(3) and (4)

4.23

Local authorities cannot use this section, but children can use it, as well as adults.

1995 Act, s.11(5)

4.24

The principles outlined in Chapter 2 apply to all decisions made by the court under this section. This includes taking account of children's religious persuasion, racial, cultural and linguistic heritage. See Chapter 2, paragraph 2.8.

1995 Act, s.11(7) and (10)

4.25

The law relating to children before the 1995 Act talked about "custody". The term in the 1995 Act is "residence" although it does **not** mean the same thing. A residence order may be granted to a parent who has responsibilities and rights already, **or** it may be granted to someone who does not have any responsibilities and rights to begin with, such as a grandparent or unmarried father.

1995 Act, s.11(12)

4.26

If a residence order is granted to a parent with responsibilities and rights, in a divorce action or the like, the order simply says where the child is to live. It does not take away the non-residential parent's responsibilities and rights, apart from residence, unless the court also orders this for particular reasons. The idea is to encourage parents to work together for their children. This means that the two parents with responsibilities are be expected to continue to carry these out, even if they are separated or divorced. They both still have rights too.

1995 Act, s.11(11)

4.27

If a residence order is granted to a person who does not already have responsibilities and rights, the order allows that person to have all the responsibilities and rights that are needed to care properly for the child. It does not, however, take responsibilities and rights away from anyone else who already has them, unless and only to the extent the court specifically orders that.

1995 Act, s.11(11) and (12)

4.28

Because the principle of minimum necessary intervention applies in these decisions, courts should not grant orders to disputing parents just because parents want them. Courts have to be satisfied, taking the child's welfare as paramount, that the orders wanted are necessary for the children and that it is better to make the orders than not to do so. This represented a move away from giving custodial rights to one parent in a dispute and leaving the other parent with a feeling of very little involvement.

1995 Act, s.11(7)(a)

Interdicts and enforcement

4.29

As has already been mentioned, s.11 orders can include interdicts about children, including an interdict to prevent a child being removed from someone's care, if this is necessary to protect the child.

1995 Act, s.11(2)(f)

4.30

Orders made in Scotland in relation to children are recognised and may be enforced in other parts of the United Kingdom. Orders made elsewhere in the United Kingdom are also recognised and can be enforced in Scotland.

1986 Act

Responsibilities and rights for children "looked after" by the local authority

4.31

The responsibilities of the local authorities themselves for "looked after" children are dealt with in Chapter 9. However, there is the issue of what parents' responsibilities and rights are when children are "looked after" by a local authority, either on a voluntary basis or because of a supervision requirement from the children's hearing system. The position depends on the basis on which children are "looked after".

4.32

Unlike the position in England and Wales in care orders under the 1989 Act, local authorities do **not** acquire responsibilities and rights for "looked after" children except when they obtain PROs. For most "looked after" children, they have no responsibilities and rights and this affects day-to-day issues for children, such as medical consent and holiday arrangements. Local authorities do have duties (see Chapter 9) but not parental responsibilities and rights.

4.33

If a child is accommodated by the local authority, this is a "voluntary" arrangement and parents do not lose responsibilities and rights. If they have any dispute with the local authority, they can ask for the child to be returned to them.

1995 Act, s.25

4.34

If a child is subject to a supervision requirement in the hearing system, under s.70 of the 1995 Act, the child may be at home or away from home. If the child is at home, the responsibilities and rights are only interfered with to the extent that the local authority have a responsibility to supervise.

However, if a child is away from home on a supervision requirement, the parents' responsibilities and rights will be interfered with to some extent. They cannot demand the return of the child. If there is a requirement, the courts generally should not use s.11 to make orders contradicting the requirement about contact.

1995 Act, s.3(4) and P v P 2000 SLT 781 (29 February 2000)

4.35

If someone wants to use s. 11 to obtain a residence order for a child on a supervision requirement away from home, the court may grant such an order but the supervision requirement still takes precedence. If the court grants an order to the carer named by the hearing system (e.g. a grandparent) then there is no conflict. If an order is granted to someone with whom the child does not live, it cannot be enforced unless and until the supervision requirement is terminated or varied to name that person.

1995 Act, s.3(4) and P v P 2000 SLT 781 (29 February 2000)

Section 54 referrals

4.36

Section 54 1995 Act allows any civil court in a wide range of cases, including adoption, to refer a child to the children's reporter. The court finds grounds for referral established, and asks the reporter to consider the case. It is up to the reporter to decide whether to refer the child to a hearing. This is now the way in which a court dealing with private law cases refers a child into the pubic law system if the court is concerned about the arrangements for the child. See Chapter 11 on the hearing system.

1995 Act, s.54

4.37

The courts no longer have powers to place a child directly into the care of the local authority or under supervision in private law cases, as they did before the 1995 Act came into force in 1996 and 1997.

1995 Act, Schedule 5

5 The 2001 Act and the Care Commission

This chapter deals with the Regulation of Care (Scotland) Act 2001, the systems it set up and the establishment of the Scottish Commission for the Regulation of Care and the Scottish Social Services Council.

The 2001 Act

5.1

This replaced the existing structures and systems for the registration of a wide range of care services in the health and social care sectors. It also established two new bodies, the Scottish Commission for the Regulation of Care, the Care Commission, and the Scottish Social Services Council, the Council.

5.2

The 14 "care services" covered by the 2001 Act are listed in s. 2(1). They include support services, care homes, secure accommodation, adoption, fostering, childminding and day care of children. Some of the services listed are only provided for children, like adoption, fostering and day care, but others are for all ages, such as care homes.

2001 Act, s.2(1)

5.3

All the services listed have to be registered with and inspected by the Care Commission – see paragraph 5.7 below. Some of the services, like residential schools, childminding and nursing homes, were previously registered and inspected by local authorities. Other services, particularly adoption and fostering, were not registered and inspected at all, or only in a limited way. On 1 April 2002, the Care Commission took over existing local authority duties to register and inspect a range of services. Since then, the registration and inspection of other services have been introduced. All adoption and fostering services have had to be registered with the Care Commission since 1 April 2004.

2001 Act, s. 7, s.33 and s.25.

5.4

There are a variety of regulations and orders made under the 2001 Act. These are not specific to one type of care service and include provisions for:

* commencement and transitional provisions;
* fees;
* registration of services; and
* requirements to be complied with by providers of care services.

5.5

As part of the system of registration and inspection, Scottish Ministers are obliged to publish National Care Standards for the various care services. The Standards must be taken into account by the Care Commission in all its decisions about registration, inspection and any proceedings under the 2001 Act.

2001 Act, s.5

5.6

The main National Care Standards for services for or including children are:

* Adoption Standards – see Chapter 13;
* Care at home;
* Care homes for children and young people;
* Childcare agencies – see Chapter 6;
* Early education and child care up to 16 – see Chapter 6;

- Fostering Standards – see Chapter 10;
- School care accommodation services.

The Standards are available on the Care Commission's website – see Further Reading.

The Scottish Commission for the Regulation of Care

5.7

The Care Commission came into operation in April 2002. It is the body responsible for the regulation, registration and inspection of all the care services in Scotland listed in the 2001 Act. It also deals with complaints about services and enforcement of Standards and conditions.

2001 Act, s.1, s.7, s.33, s.25 and s.6

The Scottish Social Services Council

5.8

The Council is responsible for the registration in Scotland of all social workers and social service workers. The Register of Social Service Workers in Scotland opened on 1 April 2003 for all workers with a Diploma in Social Work (DipSW) or equivalent qualification. Qualified social workers had to register by 1 May 2005 in order to meet the deadline for protection of the title of "social worker" which came into effect on 1 September 2005. No final date for registration of other workers has been set.

2001 Act, s.44 and s.52

5.9

The Council must also promote high standards of behaviour and practice among social services workers and in education and training. There are UK-wide Codes developed by the Council and the equivalent regulatory bodies in the rest of the UK. These lay down the standards of conduct and practice people can expect from social services workers and their employers. All workers and employers are expected to adhere to the Codes.

2001 Act, s.43 and s.53

6 Private arrangements

This chapter deals with private care arrangements which parents and families may make for their children at home, with relatives or with other people. Childminding and day care of children were formerly covered by the 1989 Act and are now regulated by the 2001 Act.

Arrangements at home

6.1

If parents make arrangements directly with a carer for babysitting or child care in their own home, **without** the involvement of a childcare agency, there are no controls over these. The 2001 Act does not cover such arrangements. However, a carer and/or the parents could be liable criminally if the arrangements are inadequate.

1937 Act, s.12

6.2

When child carers do not have parental responsibilities and rights, they still have a general duty to safeguard the children's welfare. They may also be able to consent to medical treatment in certain circumstances, provided they are at least 16 and if the children are too young to consent and they have no reason to believe the parents would refuse to consent.

1995 Act, s.5

6.3

It is not an offence to leave children under 16 unattended, but if harm or neglect is suffered by the children, the people who left them unattended may be charged with a criminal offence. This applies to parents and any other carers who are 16 or over.

1937 Act, s.12

Arrangements with family

6.4

If parents make arrangements for a child to be cared for by a close relative, there is no regulatory control or involvement. If the relative is not a close one and the care is for less than 28 days, there is no regulatory control. If the care is for more than 28 days, then it will be a private fostering arrangement and the local authority must be notified. See Chapter 10, paragraphs 10.11–10.19.

Childminding

6.5

Childminding was formerly regulated under the 1989 Act and is now one of the care services listed in the 2001 Act. Childminders must therefore register with the Care Commission (see Chapter 5). There are conditions in regulations for registration and it may be refused. There is an annual registration and inspection fee. In addition, the Care Commission must inspect the premises which are used for childminding and the arrangements.

2001 Act, s.2(1), s.7 and s.25

6.6

A childminder is someone who looks after 'one or more children on domestic premises for reward'. It is not childminding when a child is cared for by a parent, relative, someone with parental responsibilities and rights or a public or private foster carer.

2001 Act, s.2(17) and (18)

6.7

The Standards that apply to childminding are the National Care Standards: Early education and child care up to the age of 16.

6.8

A nanny is not a childminder if she or he is looking after a child in the home of her or his employer. However, if he or she has been supplied or introduced to the parents by a childcare agency, that is a childcare agency service, which is regulated by the 2001 Act. See paragraphs 6.11 and 6.12 below.

2001 Act, s.2(7)

Day care

6.9

Day care was formerly regulated under the 1989 Act and is now a care service in the 2001 Act. It is defined in the 2001 Act as a service provided for children and which involves 'any form of care supervised by a responsible person' during the day in non-domestic premises. Providers must register with the Care Commission, which may impose certain conditions. These include specifying the number of children able to be cared for and the number of helpers. Registration may be refused or cancelled. The Care Commission must inspect daycare services.

2001 Act, s.2(1) and (20), s.7 and s.25

6.10

Day care can include nursery classes, crèches, after-school groups and playgroups if provided for more than two hours in a day and more than six days in a year. They may be run by the public, private or voluntary sectors. The Standards are the National Care Standards: Early education and child care up to 16.

2001 Act, s.2(21) and (22)

Childcare agencies

6.11

Childcare agencies are care services defined in the 2001 Act as services supplying or introducing to parents child carers to look after a child or young person up to the age of 16, wholly or mainly in their homes. They may include nanny agencies, home-based childcare services and sitter services. The agencies may be managed by private, voluntary or local authority providers. The service may or may not be for reward.

2001 Act, s.2(1) and (7)

6.12

The supply or introduction of child carers through a childcare agency is regulated under the 2001 Act and the provisions about them came into force on 1 April 2003. Agencies must register with the Care Commission, which may impose certain conditions. Registration may be refused or cancelled. The Care Commission must inspect childcare agencies. The Standards are the National Care Standards: Childcare agencies.

2001 Act, s.7 and s.25

6.13

When parents enter into arrangements directly with a child carer for babysitting or child care in their home, without involving an agency, the arrangements are not subject to regulation under the 2001 Act. See paragraph 6.1 above.

Private fostering

6.14

Private fostering is care of a child provided:
* by an individual who is **not** a close relative; and

- on a private basis by arrangement between the parents and the individual; and
- for a period of 28 days or more.

Private fostering is covered by the 1984 Act and the 1985 Regs. It must be distinguished from public foster care arranged by the local authority, where the local authority make such arrangements and place a child with approved foster carers. Public fostering makes a child a "looked after" child. Public and private fostering are dealt with in Chapter 10.

1984 Act; 1985 Regs

7 General local authority duties to children

This chapter deals with the general duties of local authorities to all children in their area, and in particular towards children "in need". These provisions are concerned with what is generally seen as preventive work. Local authority duties to "looked after" children are dealt with in Chapter 9.

7.1

The duties in this chapter and which are in the 1995 Act are duties on the whole local authority and not just on the social work department. See Chapter 2, paragraph 2.14.

1995 Act, s.93(1)

General welfare duty

7.2

Local authorities are under a statutory duty to promote social welfare generally for everyone over 18 in their area, by giving advice, guidance and assistance. Under these provisions, they may give assistance in kind and in cash to families.

1968 Act, s.12 as amended by the 1995 Act, Schedule 4, para 15(11)

Children's Services Plans

7.3

Local authorities are obliged to produce a Children's Services Plan for their area covering all the "relevant services" they have to provide for children. These are not only the duties and powers under the 1995 Act, but also other ones in a range of legislation, including the 1984 Act and the 1978 Act.

1995 Act, s.19

Children "in need"

7.4

The 1995 Act introduced a definition of children "in need" as being children for whom as wide a range as possible of services should be provided, to promote their welfare and to assist them to develop. The main provision is in s. 22 of the 1995 Act, but that section does not replace the general duty to do preventive work in s. 12 of the 1968 Act.

1995 Act, s.22

7.5

In practice, local authorities use their powers under s. 22 to provide services to children "in need", but may also use their general duties under s.12 of the 1968 Act as well.

7.6

Local authorities must safeguard and promote the welfare of children in their area who are "in need". The services provided under this duty may be for:
- the child; or
- his or her family, if the services help the child; or
- any other member of the family, if the services help the child.

These services may be in cash or kind.

1995 Act, s.22(1) and (3)

7.7

The definition of "in need" is very wide, and each local authority must have instructions and guidance so that individual decisions can be made about children and families. A child will be considered "in need" if he or she is:
- unlikely to achieve or maintain or have the opportunity of achieving or

maintaining a reasonable standard of health or development unless he or she receives services; or

- his or her health or development is likely significantly to be impaired or further impaired unless services are provided; or
- he or she is disabled; or
- he or she is adversely affected by the disability of any other person in the family.

1995 Act, s.93(4)(a)

Disabled children and children affected by disability

7.8

The definition of "in need" means that children who are adversely affected by the disability of someone else in the family are covered, as well as children who are themselves disabled. This covers children who act as carers for others in the family. The duties about "carers' assessments" (see paragraph 7.11 below) apply to child carers as well as to adult ones.

1995 Act, s.24(1) as amended

7.9

Disability is defined as 'chronically sick or disabled or [suffering] from mental disorder' (within the meaning of the Mental Health (Care and Treatment) (Scotland) Act 2003).

1995 Act, s.23(2)

7.10

When a child is "in need" because of disability, the parents may ask for an assessment of the child or anyone else in the family, to establish the child's needs so far as attributable to the disability. The local authority must carry out this assessment if it is requested. They must take account of the views of the child, parents and any carer who is providing "substantial" care to the disabled person; and take account of the "substantial" care when that is provided.

1995 Act, s.23(3) and (4)

7.11

Anyone providing "substantial" care for a disabled child (including another child) can also ask for a "carer's assessment" of his or her ability to provide the care. The local authority must carry out this assessment if they consider that the child should or may receive services as a child "in need". When a child is "in need" because he or she is disabled, and the carer is providing "substantial" care, the local authority must tell him or her about being entitled to a "carer's assessment".

1995 Act, s.24(1) and (1A) and s.24A

Day care for children in need

7.12

A local authority have a duty to provide appropriate day care for children "in need" in their area. The duty covers children:
*   during the day if they are under five; **or**
*   after school **and** during holidays if they attend school.

See Chapter 6 for general arrangements about day care.

1995 Act, s.27

8 Child protection

This chapter briefly outlines the child protection system, the three orders in the Children (Scotland) Act 1995 used for the purposes of child protection, and the provisions of POCSA 2003.

Child protection

8.1

Most of the child protection system is organised on the basis of Guidance from the Scottish Executive and is not contained in statutes. The Guidance requires there to be local Child Protection Committees with inter-disciplinary membership, and local child protection policies and guidelines. These cover such matters as what the different agencies should do when they have concerns about children, child protection case conferences, and when children should be "registered" on the local Child Protection Register. Social work departments and the police are expected to be the lead agencies and all agencies should work co-operatively.

8.2

When local authorities have emergency concerns about a child, they should consider the use of the various orders available under the 1995 Act – see below. They may also, as may any agency or person, refer a child to the children's reporter. If a local authority or the police think that a child may need compulsory measures of supervision, they must refer to the reporter. See Chapter 11, paragraph 11.8.

Child assessment order (CAO)

8.3

This order was a new introduction to the law of Scotland in the 1995 Act. It allows local authorities (and only local authorities) to apply to the sheriff to grant an order 'for an assessment of the state of a child's health or development or of the way in which he has been treated'. The sheriff has to be satisfied that:

- the local authority have 'reasonable cause to suspect' that the child is being treated or neglected so as to be suffering or likely to suffer 'significant harm'; **and**
- an assessment is necessary in order to find out if there is 'reasonable cause to believe that there is or has been such treatment of the child'; **and**
- the assessment will not be carried out unless the order is granted.

1995 Act, s.55(1)

8.4

The order can last for a maximum of seven days and must specify the date when it starts and the length of time it is to last. It can authorise the production of the child to anyone for the purposes of assessment. It can allow any type of assessment. One obvious use is for medical assessment, but the order is not restricted to this.

1995 Act, s.55(3) and (4)

8.5

There are no regulations regarding these orders, but a child is "looked after" by the local authority if the order states that the child is to be away from home for the assessment. If the child is "looked after", the local authority have duties to the child, as listed in Chapter 9.

8.6

There are court rules about applying for CAOs. They cannot be obtained on an "emergency" basis, that is, without giving any notice to a family. They can, however, be obtained on fairly short notice such as three or seven days. If parents wish to oppose an application for an order, they appear before the sheriff, who hears both sides of the application.

AS 1997, rr.3.25–3.28

8.7

When a CAO application is made, a sheriff must grant a CPO instead of a CAO, if he or she thinks that the conditions for a CPO are satisfied.

1995 Act, s.55(2)

Child protection order (CPO)

8.8

This order replaced the "place of safety" formerly obtained under s. 37 of the 1968 Act. It was therefore not a new remedy, but the CPO has different procedures.

1995 Act, ss.57–60

8.9

Anyone may apply for a CPO, including local authorities. Almost all applications are by local authorities. All applications must go to the sheriff whose decision is bound by the HRA 1998. There are two different tests depending on who is applying.

8.10

If an application is made by "any person" (including the local authority), the test is:
• that there are reasonable grounds to believe that a child is being treated

or neglected so as to suffer 'significant harm' or will suffer such harm if not removed to and kept in a place of safety, or kept safely where he or she is; **and**

* an order is necessary to protect the child.

1995 Act, s.57(1)

8.11

If an application is made by a local authority, they may **either** satisfy the above test **or** the alternative. The alternative test is:

* that the local authority have reasonable grounds to suspect that the child is being or will be treated or neglected so as to suffer 'significant harm'; **and**
* that they are making enquiries to investigate this; **and**
* that the enquiries are being frustrated because access to the child is unreasonably denied and they need access 'as a matter of urgency'.

1995 Act, s.57(2)

8.12

A local authority may use either test, but anyone else can only use the test in paragraph 8.10.

8.13

Again, there are court rules about applying for CPOs. They are dealt with on an emergency basis and notice is not given to the family in advance. Instead, if the sheriff is satisfied and grants an order, the local authority or other applicant must immediately serve on or give to the family a copy of the order. This should be done when they remove the child or tell the family that the child is not being removed from the place of safety where she or he already is. If the sheriff considers the child is old enough, a copy of the order will also be given to the child, with a special "child friendly" form.

AS 1997, rr.3.29–3.33

8.14

If a CPO is granted, the child becomes a "looked after" child (see Chapter 9). Also, the child must be referred immediately to the children's reporter, who must decide whether he or she will take the case forward to a children's hearing. There are very complicated rules about times within which hearings must be held, and failure to stick to the rules means that the CPO will fall. Decisions about whether the child continues to stay on an order are made by the children's hearing members and/or the sheriff, depending on whether the family exercises its rights to ask the sheriff to reconsider the case. A CPO lasts for a maximum of eight working days. At the end of this time, if the case is proceeding, there must be a hearing at which grounds for referral are put and a decision made as to whether the child is to continue to be "away from home" on a hearing warrant. See Chapter 11.

1995 Act, s.59 and s.60

Emergency protection

8.15

There are arrangements for sheriffs to be available for applications to be heard at any time, including out of hours. If, however, a local authority or other persons are unable to present an application to a sheriff, they may seek emergency protection from a Justice of the Peace. The Justice has to be satisfied on the same terms as the sheriff, and also that it is not "practicable in the circumstances" for a sheriff to deal with the matter. If such emergency protection is obtained, it falls if not implemented within 12 hours. In addition, it can only last for a maximum of 24 hours, by which time the matter must be put before a sheriff with a CPO application, unless the child goes home.

1995 Act, s.61

8.16

The police have a similar power to give emergency protection for up to 24 hours.

1995 Act, s.61(5)–(8)

Exclusion order (EO)

8.17

Like CAOs, EOs were introduced by the 1995 Act and represented a new remedy. They allow a person to be removed from the family home if the child is at risk, as an alternative to removing the child from home. Only the local authority can apply and the application must be made to a sheriff.

8.18

The sheriff must be satisfied that:
- the child has suffered, is suffering or is likely to suffer 'significant harm' because of the behaviour, threats, etc. of 'the named person'; **and**
- that it is necessary to make an EO against the 'named person' to protect the child, this being a better safeguard for the child than taking him or her away from home; **and**
- that if the order is made, there will be an 'appropriate person' in the house to care for the child and anyone else there.

1995 Act, s.76(2)

8.19

Again, there are court rules about these applications. An application for an EO may either be on an "emergency basis", without notice, or be heard after notice has been given to the family and to the 'named person'.

AS 1997, rr.3.34–3.40

8.20

A sheriff may grant an EO without giving notice to the 'named person', but it may be difficult to satisfy a sheriff that this should be done.

1995 Act, s.76(4)

8.21

Another practical difficulty is that the local authority, in applying for the order, and the sheriff, in granting it, have to be satisfied that there is an 'appropriate person' and that he or she will fully protect the child and anyone else in the house, and not simply allow the 'named person' back into the house.

1995 Act, s.76(2)(c)

8.22

An EO can last for a maximum of six months. When the sheriff initially grants the order it will probably be as an interim order, whether notice has been given or not. An interim order is as good as a full order, unless it has been granted on an emergency basis. In that case, there must be another hearing within three days, after notice has been given to the 'named person'. Conditions and powers of arrest may be attached to an EO or interim EO after notice.

1995 Act, s.79, s.77 and s.78; AS 1997, r.3.36

8.23

When an application is made for an EO, the sheriff may grant a CPO instead of the EO if satisfied that the conditions for a CPO are met.

1995 Act, s.76(8)

POCSA 2003

8.24

This came largely into force in early 2005. Under it, Scottish Ministers must keep a List of people who are unsuitable to work with children. No one on it may work with children on a paid or unpaid basis. As a result, from 2005, all people who start to work with children, in a paid or unpaid capacity, will have to have criminal records checks carried out on them before they can do the work, to check that they are not on the List. Many people were already being checked for employment, approval as foster carers or adoptive parents or in other capacities but the effect of the Act is to make checks mandatory. Voluntary organisations do not have to pay for the checks. The checks are carried out by Disclosure Scotland. See Chapter 2, paragraphs 2.15 and 2.16.

8.25

POCSA 2003 also has complex rules imposing duties on employers and voluntary organisations to notify Scottish Ministers when they think the behaviour of an employee, former employee, volunteer or former volunteer raises concerns. It is up to Scottish Ministers to decide if individuals should be put on the List. Anyone convicted of certain offences after the Act came into force automatically goes on the List.

9 Local authority responsibilities for "looked after" children

This chapter deals with "looked after" children, who they are, and what responsibilities local authorities have.

"Looked after" children

9.1

"Looked after" children is the phrase that was introduced by the 1995 Act and replaced references to children "in care". It should be noted that the definition of "looked after" child is wider than the various definitions of "in care" and is different from the definitions in the law for England and Wales.

Who are "looked after" children?

9.2

The definition of a "looked after" child is in s. 17(5) of the 1995 Act. A child is "looked after" when she or he is:

- accommodated under s. 25; **or**
- subject to a supervision requirement from the hearing system (see Chapter 11) in terms of section 70; **or**
- the subject of an order, authorisation or warrant issued by a sheriff or a children's hearing in terms of Chapters 2 and 3 of Part II of the 1995 Act. These include CPOs and any CAO where the child is away from home (see Chapter 8); **or**
- the subject of a PRO in terms of s. 86 (see Chapter 12); **or**
- the subject of any order made when he or she is transferred to Scotland from another part of the United Kingdom having been the subject of a care order, etc. – s.33.

1995 Act, s.17(6), s.25, s.70, Chapters 2 and 3 of Part II, s.86, and s.33

9.3

This is a definitive list. If the authority for the placement or keeping of a child is not on this list, the child is not "looked after". The list **does not** include children who:
* are accommodated by virtue purely of educational placements; **or**
* have been freed for adoption; **or**
* are accommodated in a refuge provided under s. 38 of the 1995 Act.

Duties of the local authority

9.4

There are a wide variety of duties owed by the local authority to "looked after" children. These duties are contained in the 1995 Act and the various Regulations made thereunder, particularly the Arrangements to Look After Children (Scotland) Regulations 1996 – the LA Regs 1996.

9.5

The duties listed in the 1995 Act are to:
* safeguard and promote the child's welfare as paramount concern;
* make such use of services for the children as reasonable parents would;
* promote regular personal relations and direct contact between the child and anyone with parental responsibilities, **having regard to** the child's welfare as paramount **and** what is practical and appropriate;
* provide advice and assistance to a child, with a view to preparing him or her for when he or she is no longer "looked after";
* find out and take account of the views of the child, his or her parents and others with responsibilities and rights or an interest in the child, before making any decisions about the child;
* take account of the child's religious persuasion, racial origin and cultural and linguistic background before making any decisions;
* carry out a review of each child's case at set intervals; and
* provide advice, guidance and assistance to any child who was "looked after" at the date on which he or she could leave school, is no

longer "looked after" by a local authority and is under 19 (see paragraph 9.11).

1995 Act, s.17(1)(a), (b) and (c), (3) and (4), s.31(1) and s.29 as amended by the 2001 Act

9.6

Further details of these and other duties are contained in the LA Regs 1996. These make some distinctions between children who are "looked after" and placed (i.e. are away from home and placed by the local authority) and children who are simply "looked after" and remain at home. In particular, the LA Regs 1996 cover:

- how and when children's cases are to be reviewed;
- what requires to be in care plans for "looked after" children and how these are reviewed; and
- the duty that before or as soon as possible after children become "looked after" **and** placed, they must have a medical assessment to ascertain their medical needs.

LA Regs 1996, reg.8–9, reg.3–6 and reg.13

9.7

Reviews for "looked after" and placed children must be within six weeks of the placement; then within a further three months; and then within every six months thereafter. Children who are merely "looked after" must have their cases reviewed first of all within three months; and thereafter every six months. Care plan requirements are slightly increased for children who are "looked after" and placed, as opposed to children who are "looked after". There is no requirement for a medical examination for a child who is "looked after" and not placed.

9.8

The LA Regs 1996 cover other matters such as notifications of incidents and establishments of records. In addition, there are separate regulations for "looked after" children who are in foster care, in residential establishments and in secure accommodation. For further information about public fostering, see Chapter 10.

Provision of accommodation

9.9

The local authority have a duty to accommodate children for whom no one has parental responsibilities, or who are lost or abandoned, or who cannot be cared for by their normal carer, temporarily or permanently, for whatever reason. Such care is often referred to as "voluntary" care, as it comes about by agreement with parents or carers, or a complete absence of any parent or carer, not because of an order from a court or a hearing. The local authority must provide such accommodation for children up to 18 where they fall into the above categories. Children accommodated in this way are "looked after" and placed.

1995 Act, s.25

Respite care

9.10

This term is not specifically mentioned in the 1995 Act or the LA Regs 1996, but the effect of these is that all respite placements which are planned by a local authority and which last for more than 24 hours at a time are treated as "looked after" placements in terms of s.25 (provision of accommodation, see para 9.9). Such arrangements are therefore regulated and the children are treated as "looked after" and placed children. If they are given respite in a family, the carers must be approved foster carers (see Chapter 10, paragraph 10.7 about foster care approval). There is, however, some modification of the requirements for reviews and medical examinations. Only one medical examination is required at the beginning of a series of placements. These provisions apply to children who receive respite care which lasts for more than 24 hours and is arranged by a local authority, whatever the reason for the respite. This includes children with disabilities.

LA Regs 1996, reg.17

Aftercare

9.11

Local authorities have "aftercare" duties to certain young people when they cease to be "looked after". When young people cease to be "looked after" at or after the age they could leave school (i.e. 15½ to 16½), and whether or not they do leave school, local authorities have duties under s.29 of the 1995 Act as amended by the 2001 Act and the Leaving Care Regs 2003.

1995 Act, s.29; Leaving Care Regs 2003

10 Fostering

This chapter briefly outlines the law about fostering, including the different types of fostering.

Types of fostering

10.1

There are basically two types of fostering:
- public fostering, governed by the 1995 Act and the F Regs 1996; **and**
- private fostering, governed by the 1984 Act and the 1985 Regs.

1995 Act; F Regs 1996; 1984 Act; 1985 Regs

10.2

The 2001 Act lists fostering as one of the services covered. Section s. 1(15) says:
- The "Scottish public fostering service" is the service mentioned in s. 2(14)(a) **and** (b). This is local authorities' own direct service provision under s. 26(1) of the 1995 Act **and** their arrangements with voluntary organisations. Both of these services are for children "looked after" by authorities in terms of the 1995 Act.
- The "Scottish private fostering service" is the service mentioned in s. 2(14)(c). This is the range of duties which local authorities have under the 1984 Act.

2001 Act, s.2(1), (14) and (15); 1995 Act; 1984 Act

10.3

There is confusion about the differences between the two types of fostering, and how private fostering works. There are no reliable statistics about how many private fostering arrangements there are in Scotland.

10.4

Both fostering services are regulated and covered by the 2001 Act. From 1 April 2004, all public fostering services run by local authorities and by voluntary organisations have had to be registered with and inspected by the Care Commission. In addition, local authorities' private fostering services, their duties under the 1984 Act and 1985 Regs, have had to be registered with and inspected by the Care Commission from that date (see Chapter 5).

2001 Act, s.2(1), s.33, s.7 and s.25

Public fostering

10.5

Public fostering is where a child is "looked after" by a local authority and they place the child in a family home. The child may be "looked after" in one of a variety of ways – see Chapter 9, paragraph 9.2. All publicly fostered children are "looked after" and are therefore covered by the local authority duties set out in the LA regs 1996. The F Regs 1996 also apply.

1995 Act, s.25 and s.26; LA Regs 1996; F Regs 1996

10.6

The F Regs 1996 cover:
- the assessment and approval of carers;
- placement in foster care;
- arrangements between local authorities and voluntary organisations; and
- record keeping.

There are also Schedules which set out the information which should be obtained on the prospective carers when they are assessed; matters to be covered in individual Foster Carer Agreements, contracts between carers and authorities, etc.; and matters to be covered in individual Foster Placement Agreements, about each child placed.

F Regs 1996

10.7

All foster carers must be assessed and approved by a local authority or a voluntary organisation. A local authority can place children with carers approved by another authority or a voluntary organisation. Each local authority must have a Fostering Panel. This Panel makes recommendations on the approval, etc. of carers.

F Regs 1996, reg.7, reg.4 and reg.5

10.8

Public foster carers do not acquire parental responsibilities and rights because of fostering arrangements. However, carers have general duties and rights in relation to the children in their care under s. 5 of the 1995 Act, and may be able to consent to medical treatment (see Chapter 6, paragraph 6.2). Foster carers who look after children who are subject to supervision requirements may also be relevant persons for the purposes of the hearing system (see Chapter 11, paragraph 11.16).

1995 Act, s.5 and s.93(2)(b)

10.9

Voluntary organisation 'means a body (other than a public or local authority) whose activities are not carried on for profit'.

1995 Act, s.93(1); F Regs 1996, reg.2(1)

10.10

Local authorities and voluntary organisations are expected to use the Fostering Standards in their work and will be inspected against them.

2001 Act, s.5

Private fostering

10.11

Private fostering is foster care provided on a private basis by arrangement between parents and someone who is **not** a close relative. As explained above, it is to be distinguished from public foster care arranged by the local authority.

10.12

Separate legislation covers private fostering arrangements. Arrangements are private fostering ones when:
* the arrangements are made by someone who has parental responsibilities and rights for the child;
* the child is placed with someone who is not a close relative or guardian;
* the child is under the compulsory school leaving age; and
* the care arrangements are for 28 days or more.

1984 Act, s.1 and s.2

10.13

Relative is defined in the 1984 Act as grandparents, brothers and sisters, uncles and aunts, whether full or half blood. So if more distant relatives care for a child for more than 28 days, that is a private fostering arrangement.

1984 Act, s.21

10.14

Where such private arrangements are made, the parent and foster carer must notify the local authority not less than two weeks before the arrangement starts, unless it is an emergency. In the case of an emergency, notification must be made within one week.

1984 Act, s.4 and s.5; 1985 Regs

10.15

When the local authority are notified, they have a duty to be satisfied about the well-being of the child. The child must be visited within one week of the placement and on a regular basis thereafter. The authority may prohibit such private arrangements, or impose conditions on the arrangements if they are not satisfied.

1984 Act, s.3, s.9 and s.10; 1985 Regs

10.16

Some people may be disqualified from being private foster carers, including those convicted of certain criminal offences and/or those who have been refused registration or removed from registration as childminders.

1984 Act, s.7

10.17

Private foster carers who are caring for children do not have parental responsibilities and rights. They have general rights of control because they are acting in the place of parents. They must usually return the child to his or her parents on request unless they have obtained some other authority to keep the child.

10.18

Private foster carers have a general obligation to safeguard and protect the child's welfare and the right to consent to medical treatment in certain circumstances (see Chapter 6, paragraph 6.2).

1995 Act, s.5

10.19

Although local authorities' private fostering services must be registered with and inspected by the Care Commission (see paragraph 10.4) there are no National Care Standards for private fostering.

11 The children's hearing system

This chapter provides some basic information about children's hearings and how they operate, including the involvement of the children's reporter, the local authority and others.

The system

11.1

The Scottish children's hearing system was introduced by the 1968 Act. It was an innovation of large proportions resulting from the Kilbrandon Report (*Children and Young Persons: Scotland* (1964), Cmnd. 2306) and replacing the former juvenile court system. The system deals with children who commit crimes and all other children with social problems. Since its introduction, children charged with crime are only dealt with in the adult system if the crime is a more serious one (see Chapter 3). Most crimes where children under 16 are charged are reported by the police to the reporter only, and not to the PF (see Chapter 3).

11.2

The system is not concerned with guilt or innocence but the welfare principle: what is in the child's best interests. This principle applies whether the child has offended or has been offended against. In other words, one system deals with both juvenile criminal justice and children's welfare.

11.3

When the system was first introduced it dealt largely with criminal cases, but over the years more and more cases have been concerned with child protection in its wider sense, as the awareness of this has increased.

11.4

The 1995 Act repealed that part of the 1968 Act dealing with the system, and re-enacted it. There were some changes to and updating of the system, taking account of the lapse of time since the 1968 Act, and also various reports, including the Clyde Enquiry into the Orkney case. Nonetheless, the essence of the hearing system as introduced in 1968 remains much the same, including the pre-eminence of the welfare principle.

11.5

Each local authority in Scotland have a panel of specially recruited lay members (a children's panel) appointed by Scottish Ministers. They are called panel members. The system of panel member selection, training and appointment is maintained by local Children's Panel Advisory Committees, one for each local authority area.

1995 Act, s.39

11.6

When a hearing is held, it must consist of three panel members, of whom one must be a man and one a woman One of the panel members with experience and appropriate training acts as the chairman, although he or she has no overriding vote. Decisions are made unanimously or by majority.

1995 Act, s.39(5)

11.7

The reporter to the children's panel or children's reporter acts in some ways like a clerk to a hearing, but he or she has many other duties throughout the wider system. Since 1 April 1996, the reporter's service has operated on a national basis as the Scottish Children's Reporter Administration (SCRA). There is a Principal Reporter and an authority reporter for every local authority area, except a few small authorities, who share one. This system is independent of and separate from the system whereby panel members are appointed.

Local Government etc. (Scotland) Act 1994

Referral to the reporter

11.8

Anyone **may** provide information or refer a child to the reporter where he or she thinks that "compulsory measures of supervision" may be necessary for the child. The local authority have a **duty** to refer if they find, after enquiries, that such measures may be necessary. The police also have a **duty** to refer and any other person **may** do so. The bulk of referrals come from the local authority, including social work and education departments, the police and health services.

1995 Act, s.53(1) & 2

11.9

Anyone making a referral will probably think about the possible grounds for referral (see paragraph 11.14 below) but the decisions about whether there are grounds, and if so, which ones, are for the reporter (see below, Reporter's duties and options). This means that, if any person or body is concerned about a child, they can refer whether or not they think there are grounds for referral.

11.10

A child in the hearing system is usually under 16. However, once a child is subject to a supervision requirement, he or she can stay in the system until the age of 18. Any child under 16 may be referred to the reporter, but if it is decided that compulsory measures are necessary, the reporter must be able to have the first hearing before the child's 16th birthday, unless he or she is already subject to a supervision requirement. This means, in practice, that the referral of a child to the reporter near his or her 16th birthday may be of little assistance to the child if the child is not already subject to a supervision requirement.

1995 Act, s.93(2)(b)

Reporter's duties and options

11.11

When a child has been referred to the reporter, he or she, after 'such… investigation… as he thinks necessary', has three options. The reporter must decide:

- that a hearing is not required and inform the child's family, etc. of this decision; **or**
- that a hearing is not necessary but that it is appropriate to refer the case to the local authority to provide 'advice, guidance and assistance' for the child in terms of services provided to children "in need" and other children; **or**
- to arrange a children's hearing because it is felt that 'compulsory measures of supervision are necessary' – in other words, some form of order seems needed.

1995 Act, s.56(1), (4)(a), (4)(b) and (6)

11.12

Where a reporter has arranged a hearing, he or she must request a report on the child from the local authority, unless one has already been done as part of the initial investigation. Further additional information can also be sought from the local authority which must provide it.

1995 Act, s.56(7)

11.13

In essence, the reporter's decision to proceed to a hearing is made on the basis that:

- the child needs compulsory measures of supervision, i.e. there is a

basis for statutory intervention, looking at the child's welfare; **and**
• there is sufficient evidence to establish one or more of the grounds for referral (see below).

1995 Act, s.65(1)

Grounds for referral

11.14

A child may be in need of compulsory measures of supervision if any one of the following conditions is satisfied. These are that the child:
a) is beyond the control of any relevant person (parent, carer, etc.);
b) is falling into bad associations or exposed to moral danger;
c) is likely to suffer unnecessarily or have his or her health or development seriously impaired because of a lack of parental care;
d) has had committed against him or her any of the offences listed in Schedule 1 to the Criminal Procedure (Scotland) Act 1995;
e) is, or is likely to become, a member of the same household as a child against whom a Schedule 1 offence has been committed;
f) is, or is likely to become, a member of the same household as a person who has committed a Schedule 1 offence;
g) is, or is likely to become, a member of the same household as someone against whom incest or related offences in the Criminal Law (Consolidation) (Scotland) Act 1995 were committed by someone else in the same household;
h) has failed to attend school regularly without reasonable excuse;
i) has committed an offence;
j) has misused alcohol or any drug, whether or not a controlled drug in terms of the Misuse of Drugs Act 1971;
k) has misused a volatile substance by deliberately inhaling its vapour;
l) is looked after by the local authority under section 25 (providing accommodation) or section 86 (PRO) and his or her behaviour is such that special measures are necessary for supervision;
m)is a child to whom subsection (2A) applies.

1995 Act, s.52(2)

11.15

The last condition or ground was inserted by the ASBA 2004. Subsection (2A) refers to a situation where the sheriff has ordered the reporter to refer to a hearing a child who is subject to an ASBO and who is not already subject to a supervision requirement. See paragraphs 11.37 to 11.43.

ASBA 2004, s.12

Relevant persons

11.16

In the 1995 Act, the term used for adults with the right to attend a children's hearing is relevant person (not "parent"). This is anyone, including a parent, who has parental responsibilities and rights, and also includes anyone who ordinarily (not by employment) has charge of or control over the child. A foster carer who is caring for a child on a supervision requirement should be treated as a relevant person. There may be a number of relevant persons. A relevant person has the right to attend the child's hearing – and a duty as well – unless the hearing is satisfied that it would be unreasonable for him or her to attend. Each relevant person also has the right to bring a representative to the hearing.

1995 Act, s.93(2)(b) and s.45(8); CH Rules r.11

Hearings

11.17

When a hearing is arranged, this could be:
- for new grounds for referral; **or**
- in continuation or review of an existing case; **or**
- both; **or**
- to deal with a child protection emergency; **or**
- to provide advice to a criminal court whether the young person is subject to a supervision requirement or not.

There are detailed rules about the preparation, running and chairing of hearings. These are in the 1995 Act and the CH Rules.

11.18

In particular, unless the hearing is an emergency one, reporters must give seven days' notice of the date, time, place, etc. to children and relevant persons, and, where grounds for referral are put, at least seven days' notice of the actual grounds themselves.

CH Rules, r.6, r.7, and r.18

11.19

A child has a right and a duty to attend his or her hearing. If, however, the grounds relate to a Schedule 1 offence, or generally it would not be in the child's interests to attend the hearing, the child may be excused from attendance. However, he or she can insist on attending even if excused. The child also has a right to bring a representative to the hearing.

1995 Act, s.45(1) and (2); CH Rules, r.11

11.20

During a hearing, panel members may exclude a relevant person and/or representative for any part of the hearing. They can do this if they feel it is necessary to do so in order to find out the views of the child, or if the presence of the person is causing or is likely to cause 'significant distress' to the child. Where someone is excluded in this way, the chairman of the hearing must explain to him or her when they return 'the substance of what has taken place'.

1995 Act, s.46

11.21

Before the hearing every relevant person should be sent all the reports prepared for the hearing. These are the same reports that are sent to panel members. There is no statutory obligation to give the child a copy of these reports, but there is a system in place for this. When the child is aged 12 or over, he or she will automatically be sent the papers unless the reporter has been advised that this would clearly be against the child's interests. When the child is under 12, the reports are not automatically sent but this can be arranged if the reporter is advised that it would be appropriate.

CH Rules, r.5(3)

11.22

As indicated, at the hearing the child and any relevant person may each be accompanied by a representative. The chairman must explain the purpose of the hearing and go over any grounds for referral. He or she must explain the substance of the reports which the panel members, the relevant person(s) and possibly the child have received. After considering the case, the panel members must reach a decision. Before the close of the hearing, the chairman must tell the child and relevant person(s)
- what the decision is;
- the reasons for it; and
- any rights of appeal against the decision.

There are also rules about written notification of the decision. The decision could be to continue the hearing (see paragraph 11.27).

CH Rules, r.20 and r.21

11.23

Generally, hearings are conducted in terms of the principles of the 1995 Act. This means that panel members must:
- have the welfare of the child as their paramount consideration;

- seek out and take account of the views of the child; and
- not make an order unless they think it is better to make one than not to do so.

1995 Act, s.16

Grounds for referral and court applications

11.24

Where a hearing has been arranged to put grounds for referral, the chairman must explain the grounds to the child and the relevant person(s). In order to proceed any further, the panel members must be satisfied that the child and relevant person(s):
- understand the grounds; **and**
- accept them wholly or in part.

1995 Act, s.65(4)

11.25

If the grounds for referral are fully understood and accepted by the child and relevant person(s), the hearing can go ahead. If the grounds are understood and accepted in part, the panel members may discharge the parts that are not accepted and proceed on the basis of what has been accepted. If the child and/or the relevant person(s) understand but do not accept the grounds for referral at all, or not enough to allow the hearing to proceed with an accepted part, the panel members must **either**:
- direct the reporter to make an application to the sheriff; **or**
- discharge the whole referral.

If the child is incapable of understanding or does not understand the grounds for referral, again, the hearing must either direct the reporter to apply to the sheriff or discharge the grounds, even if the relevant person(s) has/have accepted them in full.

1995 Act, s.65(4), (5), (6), (7) and (9)

11.26

If the grounds for referral are sent to the court, and unless the relevant person accepts them, the sheriff hears evidence on the disputed facts and makes a decision based on the normal rules of evidence. The sheriff **either**:
- finds the grounds for referral established in full or in part, and refers them back to a hearing; **or**
- finds them not established and discharges the whole case.

The sheriff has no power to make any order about the welfare of the child in relation to the grounds. The reporter conducts the proof in front of the sheriff and the burden or onus of proof is on the reporter. All grounds must be established on the "balance of probabilities" (civil standard) except where the referred child is alleged to have committed a crime, when the standard of proof is "beyond reasonable doubt" (criminal standard). The sheriff's decision is not governed by the welfare principle because it is a straight testing of the factual evidence.

1995 Act, s.68(8), (9), (10) and (3)

Disposals by hearings

11.27

When there are accepted or established grounds, or there is a review of an existing requirement, a hearing has various choices. These are:
- to discharge grounds for referral on the basis that supervision is not necessary;
- to continue the hearing for further information and/or investigation;
- to make a supervision requirement or continue or vary an existing one;
- to terminate an existing supervision requirement if it is no longer necessary, even if there are new grounds for referral.

1995 Act, s.69(1), s.70(1) and s.73(1)

11.28

A supervision requirement may contain conditions, including where a child lives, what contact the child should have with others, an order for medical examination or treatment of the child and a secure condition.

Reviews

11.29

It is and always has been an essential part of the hearing system that no supervision requirement can last for more than one year without being reviewed. If a supervision requirement is not reviewed within a year, it automatically falls.

1995 Act, s.73(2)

11.30

There are various types of reviews including those asked for by children, relevant persons and the local authority. The main reviews are where:
- the local authority consider a review is necessary;
- the local authority are planning permanent arrangements for the child (PRO or adoption) or an adoption application is proposed;
- the child wishes the requirement reviewed (provided it was made or varied more than three months before);
- a relevant person wishes the requirement reviewed (provided it was made or varied more than three months before); and
- it is more than nine months since the requirement was last reviewed, in which case the reporter arranges a hearing.

1995 Act, s.73(4), (5), (6) and (8)

11.31

There is also an automatic review when the reporter puts new grounds for referral to a child who is already subject to a supervision requirement.

1995 Act, s.65(3)

11.32

The need for there to be a review when the local authority are planning for permanence means that hearing members must discuss plans for long-term care and adoption and give their opinion on them.

1995 Act, s.73(13)

Appeals

11.33

There are rights of appeal within the hearing system, **either** when a final decision is made **or** when a warrant is issued. If a final decision is made by a hearing, the child and/or relevant person(s) may appeal to the sheriff within three weeks of the decision. The sheriff dealing with the appeal may:
- uphold the decision; **or**
- overturn the decision and discharge the supervision requirement; **or**
- send the case back to the panel members for them to reconsider it; **or**
- substitute his or her own supervision requirement for the one made by the hearing.

If the appeal is against a warrant, it is heard very quickly and the warrant is either upheld or overturned.

1995 Act, s.51

11.34

There is a further right of appeal from the sheriff to the Sheriff Principal or straight to the Court of Session. This can be against **either** a sheriff's appeal decision about a supervision requirement **or** against a sheriff's finding that grounds for referral are established or not established. The reporter has a right to appeal at this stage, as well as the child and/or relevant person(s). If an appeal is made to the Sheriff Principal, it is possible to appeal again to the Court of Session, with the leave of the Sheriff Principal.

1995 Act, s.51(11) and (12)

Emergency situations and warrants

11.35

Children come before hearings in a variety of emergency situations. For example, the child may be the subject of a CPO (see Chapter 8), in which case there are strict and complicated timetables within which the reporter (if a hearing is necessary) must bring the case to the hearing, and the panel members look at the situation. Or a child may be detained by the police as a result of criminal allegations against him or her, and then be released to the reporter for an emergency hearing. Or a child may be found by the police after panel members have issued a warrant to find a child, and he or she is then brought to an emergency hearing for a short-term decision.

1995 Act, s.59 and s. 60, s.63 and s.45

11.36

When a hearing meets on an emergency basis it is not usually able to make a final decision. It is, however, allowed to authorise a child's detention for short periods of time, until final arrangements can be made, further investigation can be carried out and/or matters can be taken to court. There is a complicated system of orders and warrants in the 1995 Act, but basically a hearing can issue a number of warrants for up to 22 days each, allowing detention of any child. To issue a warrant, it must be satisfied that it is necessary for the child's welfare or that the child will fail to attend a subsequent hearing if there is no warrant. There is a right of appeal against any warrant. When an appeal is lodged, it must be heard within three days. The sheriff either upholds the warrant or overturns it, in which case the child returns home. In some circumstances, a sheriff can also grant warrants.

1995 Act, s.59 and s.60, s.63, s.45, s.66 and s. 69, s.51, s.67 and s.68

Antisocial Behaviour etc. (Scotland) Act 2004

11.37

This Act introduced a number of provisions which affect children and young people and which may involve the reporter, hearings and/or the courts. The provisions are not really part of the hearing system, but it is convenient to mention them here. They include allowing sheriffs to make antisocial behaviour orders (ASBOs) in relation to young people over 12 with or without referring the child to the reporter; allowing courts to make parenting orders; allowing courts and hearings to "tag" young people under 16; allowing hearings to impose duties on local authorities in supervision requirements; and allowing Sheriffs Principal to order local authorities to perform these duties when they are in breach of them.

11.38

Local authorities may apply to the sheriff for ASBOs for anyone who is 12 or over. If the person for whom the ASBO is sought is under 16, the sheriff must ask for a hearing to give advice, to see if the ASBO is "necessary". It is an offence to breach an ASBO, but no one under 16 can be imprisoned for that. When an ASBO is made for someone under 16, the sheriff may also ask the reporter to arrange a hearing. This will be on grounds, already established, in s. 52(2)(m) (see paragraphs 11.14 and 11.15) if the young person is not already subject to a supervision requirement. If the young person is already subject to a supervision requirement, the reporter must fix a review hearing if the sheriff asks for one.

ASBA 2004, s.4(1), (2) and (4), s .9, s.10 and s.12

11.39

A parenting order under the ASBA 2004 requires a person to comply with the requirements in it and to attend counselling or guidance sessions. When a court is considering parenting orders, the child's welfare is the paramount consideration.

ASBA 2004 s.103(1) and s.109

11.40

A sheriff may make a parenting order when he or she makes an ASBO in respect of someone under 16. This can be done if the sheriff thinks an 'order is desirable in the interest of preventing the child from engaging in further antisocial behaviour'. There also have to be local arrangements for parenting order compliance.

ASBA 2004, s.1

11.41

Parenting orders can also be made on the application of a local authority or the reporter, if there are local arrangements. Courts and hearings can direct the reporter to consider applying for an order. The court has to be satisfied about certain conditions before granting orders. There are provisions about reviews, variations and failures to comply.

ASBA 2004, s.102, s.114, s.116 (new s. 75A in the 1995 Act), s. 105, s.107 and s.109

11.42

Hearings and courts can make restriction of liberty orders, or "tagging" orders, for young people under 16.

ASBA 2004, s.135 and s.121

11.43

A hearing can impose a duty on a local authority in a supervision requirement, to help a child comply. If the hearing feel that the local authority are not complying with the duty, they may authorise the reporter to apply to the Sheriff Principal about the breach. The Sheriff Principal may make an order requiring the local authority to perform the duty.

ASBA 2004, s.136, inserting amendments of s.70 and s.71 and a new s.71A into the 1995 Act

12 Parental responsibilities orders (PROs)

This chapter deals with the way in which local authorities acquire parental responsibilities and rights for a child, taking them away from parents.

Applications for a PRO

12.1

In order to take over parental responsibilities and rights, a local authority must apply to the sheriff for an order transferring these to them. This procedure is in the 1995 Act and came into force on 1 April 1997. Prior to then, local authorities assumed parental rights through their committees, and this was seen as a confusing process. The court process is more open. It is only available in the sheriff court. There are no regulations for these applications and information about PROs will be found only in the 1995 Act, the sheriff court rules and the Scottish Office Guidance, Vol. 3.

1995 Act, s.86–s.89, s.16 and s.17; AS 1997 rr.2.37–2.44

12.2

Before making a PRO, the sheriff has to be satisfied that each "relevant person" either consents to the application or should have his or her consent dispensed with. "Relevant person" for these purposes is anyone who has parental responsibilities and rights in relation to the child. The definition is not the same as the one used in the hearing system (Chapter 11). The court has to be satisfied about all such persons, and it is not possible for the local authority to take away the parental responsibilities of one parent but not of another.

1995 Act, s.86(2) and (4)

12.3

The grounds for dispensing with consent are that the "relevant person":
- is not known, cannot be found or is incapable of giving agreement; **or**
- is withholding agreement unreasonably; **or**
- has persistently failed without reasonable cause **either** to safeguard and promote the child's health, development and welfare **or**, if the child is not living with him or her, to maintain personal relations and direct contact with the child on a regular basis; **or**
- has seriously ill-treated the child and re-integration into the same household is unlikely.

1995 Act, s.86(2)(b)

12.4

The grounds for dispensation are exactly the same as the grounds for dispensation with consent in adoption (see Chapter 13), although the end results of a PRO are different from that in adoption.

12.5

The rules of court for PRO applications are very similar to those in adoption cases. Forms are provided for a local authority's application. When the application is lodged, the court appoints a curator (independent person) to prepare a report on the child and his or her circumstances and a reporting officer to ask the "relevant person" whether he or she agrees, and if so, to witness the consent. The reports should be lodged within 28 days and thereafter the court will fix a hearing. If the "relevant person" is not consenting, there will be a proof hearing at which evidence may be led on one or more of the grounds for dispensing with consent.

AS 1997 r.2.38, r.2.39, r.2.40 and r.2.42

12.6

The sheriff's decision about a PRO application (apart from whether there is sufficient evidence to dispense with consent) is governed by the principles in the 1995 Act:

- that the welfare of the child is paramount;
- that the child's views shall be taken into account;
- and that no order shall be made unless it is better to make an order than not to make an order.

There is an appeal against the sheriff's decision, to the Sheriff Principal and/or the Court of Session, although there is no specific mention of this in the 1995 Act.

1995 Act, s.16

12.7

In making a PRO, the sheriff may attach any conditions. These can include contact. There is a presumption that the child will be allowed reasonable contact with the "relevant person" but it may be necessary to regulate this in the PRO. For instance, it may be necessary to impose a condition that there is no contact or that contact is supervised. Again, this matter is decided with reference to the welfare principle.

1995 Act, s.86(5) and s.88

Effects of a PRO

12.8

A PRO deprives the "relevant person" of all parental responsibilities and rights except the right to agree or disagree to the making of a freeing or adoption order. All other responsibilities and rights are transferred to the local authority.

1995 Act, s.86(3)

12.9

However, the "relevant person" retains the right to apply to court for a variation or discharge of the PRO, although he or she cannot use s. 11 of the 1995 Act. Also, there will usually be continuing contact, although this is not a parental right but rather a presumption in favour of the child.

1995 Act, s.86(5), s.88 and s.11(3) and (4)

12.10

When a child is the subject of a PRO, he or she is a "looked after" child (see Chapter 9).

1995 Act, s.17(6)(c)

Variation, discharge or termination of a PRO

12.11

Anyone with an interest, including the child, the "relevant person" and the local authority, can apply to the sheriff for variation or discharge of a PRO. Such an application will not be dealt with unless the applicant can show that there is a reason for it and a change of circumstance.

1995 Act, s.86(5)

12.12

A PRO can be discharged by the sheriff. Otherwise, the order will terminate when the child
*   becomes 18; **or**
*   is adopted or freed; **or**
*   an order is made for his or her return or certain decisions are registered under the Child Abduction and Custody Act 1985.

1995 Act, s.86(6)

13 Adoption

This chapter deals briefly with some aspects of the adoption and freeing of children in Scotland. Intercountry adoption is covered in Chapter 15.

General information

13.1

Adoption law in Scotland has been under review since 2001 and the Adoption Policy Review Group Report in June 2005 proposes considerable changes. New legislation is expected to follow, possibly in 2006, and this will be followed by new regulations and court rules. These provisions are not likely to come into force until at least 2007. In the meantime, the adoption law in England and Wales is substantially changed by the 2002 Act, which comes into force on 30 December 2005. The 2002 Act will only amend Scots law in a few matters, though there will be practice consequences in Scotland. Chapter 14 looks at the 2002 Act in more detail.

13.2

Adoption of a child is a legal process where a child's birth family is replaced in law by a new adoptive family, cutting off all legal ties and links with the birth family. The child becomes as if born into the adoptive family for almost all purposes.

1978 Act, s.39

13.3

In order for a child to be adopted, everyone with parental responsibilities and rights must either agree to the adoption, or have his or her agreement dispensed with. Agreement is dealt with in the adoption application or, in some cases, it may be done in an earlier process called freeing. If the child is 12 or over, his of her consent is also required for adoption and for freeing.

1978 Act, s.16(1), s.65, s.18(1), s.12(8) and s.18(8)

13.4

Adoption and freeing applications are dealt with in the 1978 Act. This Act was amended by the 1995 Act and all references to adoption legislation are to the 1978 Act as amended by the 1995 Act. There are regulations for adoption agencies and adoption allowances, and National Care Standards for Adoption Agencies (see Chapter 5). There are also rules of court for the sheriff court and the Court of Session, and Practice Notes for each sheriffdom, designed 'to secure the efficient management of contested proceedings' for adoption, freeing and PROs.

1978 Act; Ad Ag Regs 1996; Ad All Regs 1996; Adoption Standards; AS 1997, Ch 2; and RCS 1994, Ch 67

13.5

All local authorities have a duty to have their own adoption agency and to provide an adoption service for their area, including provision for intercountry adoption (see Chapter 15) and adoption support (see paragraph 13.36). They have to provide adoption services along with their other social work provision and with registered adoption services (see paragraph 13.7) operating in their area. Since April 2004, local authority adoption agencies must be registered with and are inspected by the Care Commission. Local authorities must also cover their adoption services in their Children's Services Plan. Adoption is one of the 'relevant services'.

1978 Act, s.1(1), (2), (3) and (3A); 2001 Act, s.33(1) and s.25(5); and 1995 Act, s.19(1) and (2)

Principles to be applied

13.6

The general principles (see Chapter 2) apply to all decisions made by courts and adoption agencies about adoption and/or freeing. These include all planning decisions by agencies. The child's welfare **throughout his or her life** is the paramount consideration. The views of the child must be sought and taken into account by agencies and courts and there must be consideration of religion, race, culture and language. Agencies and courts must also consider other options for the child, and decide on adoption only if it is the best choice. This does not mean that adoption is a last resort.

1978 Act, s.6, s.6A and s.24(3)

Adoption agencies

13.7

There are two types of adoption agencies:
- **local authority adoption agencies**: see paragraph 13.5 above;
- **registered adoption services**: these are voluntary agencies providing adoption services. They were formerly approved by the Scottish Executive under the 1978 Act, and have been registered and inspected by the Care Commission since April 2004.

The Adoption Standards apply to both types of agency. All agencies must have an adoption panel unless they do not plan for children or assess adopters.

1978 Act, s.1(1) and (5) and s.9; 2001 Act, s.5(3) and (4); Adoption Standards; Ad Ag Regs 1996, reg. 7(1) and (2).

Freeing

13.8

Freeing is a court application which can only be made by a local authority adoption agency. If a local authority agency is planning adoption for a child, it may choose to deal with parental agreement in the freeing process, before placing with adopters, or to avoid a direct dispute between birth parents and adopters over a child already placed. However, freeing is not a mandatory process and it is not necessary for a child to be freed before he or she is adopted. On the other hand, if a child is freed, there is no question of parental agreement in the adoption process, and the court is concerned with the child's welfare only.

1978 Act, s.18 and s.16(1)(a)

Types of adoption

13.9

The 1978 Act provides for two types of adoption:
* agency adoptions; and
* non-agency adoptions including relative and step-parent adoptions.

An agency adoption is where an adoption agency (see paragraph 13.7) places a child for adoption. The child will usually, but not always, be "looked after" (see Chapter 9). A relative adoption can be sought by grandparents, brothers, sisters, uncles, aunts of the full or half blood, including the father of the child and his relatives if the father was not married to the mother. In step-parent adoption, the adopter must be married to a birth parent who has parental responsibilities and rights. Most non-agency adoptions are step-parent ones.

1978 Act, s.11, s.65 and s.15(1)(aa)

13.10

Strictly speaking, no adoption should be arranged by anyone other than an adoption agency, unless it is a relative one. However, step-parent adoptions are clearly permitted and other adoptions are allowed two. In some circumstances an adoption order may be granted when the child was not placed by an agency and is not being adopted by a relative, even if money has been paid. For example, foster carers may seek to adopt a child who was placed with them under the fostering regulations, but not the adoption regulations. And intercountry adoptions are not agency ones, even though the adopters will have been assessed and approved by an agency (see Chapter 15). Courts are allowed to grant adoption orders even where money has been paid.

1978 Act, s.11(1) and s.24(2)

13.11

In practice, most adoptions are either arranged by local authorities or other agencies, or are relative or step-parent ones. The legal requirements and processes for both types of adoption are much the same, although some specific issues are different as between the two types.

Who can adopt?

13.12

There is no upper age limit for adoption, although many adoption agencies impose one, but there are lower age limits. People under 21 cannot adopt, but if the adopter is a step-parent, adoption is allowed provided the birth parent is 18, although the step-parent must be over 21. Adopters must **either** be domiciled in the UK (i.e. it is the country they are most closely associated with, even if they do not currently live here) **or** have been habitually resident in the UK for more than one year prior to the application. Where a couple are adopting, only one of them needs to be domiciled in the UK, if that is the eligibility test they are using. Adopters do not have to have British nationality to be eligible to adopt.

1978 Act, s.14 and s.15

13.13

Adopters are either a married couple or a single person. An unmarried couple (whether heterosexual or homosexual) cannot adopt together, although one of them may adopt as a single person. In step-parent adoptions from 1 April 1997 the step-parent alone has been able to adopt if he or she is married to the birth parent who agrees to the adoption. Adoption by unmarried couples in England and Wales will be allowed under the 2002 Act from 30 December 2005 (see Chapter 14). The Adoption Policy Review Group in June 2005 recommended that the law in Scotland should also be changed to allow this.

1978 Act, s.14 and s.15

Who can be adopted?

13.14

For a child to be adopted, he or she must be under 18 and unmarried. Since 1 April 1997, if an adoption petition is lodged before the child's 18th birthday, it may be dealt with and granted even after the child reaches that age. The child can be of any nationality.

1978 Act, s.12(5) and s.65

13.15

A child must have lived with the applicants or one of them before an adoption order can be granted. If the child is being adopted by a step-parent or a relative, or the adoption is an agency one, the child must be at least 19 weeks old before the adoption can be granted, **and** have lived with one or more of the applicants for the previous 13 weeks. This means that an adoption application can be lodged in court for a child under 19 weeks, and who has lived with the applicant for less than 13 weeks, but the order cannot be granted before then.

1978 Act, s.13(1)

13.16

Where an application to adopt a child is not made by a relative (as defined in the 1978 Act – see paragraph 13.9) or step-parent and the child has not been placed for adoption by an agency, the child must be at least one year old before the order is made and have lived for at least one year with the applicants or one of them. This would include foster carer applications and most but not all adoptions from abroad. The rules about this matter in intercountry adoption are covered in Chapter 15.

1978 Act, s.13(2)

Pre-court procedures – non-agency adoptions

13.17

In **all** non-agency adoptions, including relative and step-parent ones, and intercountry adoptions (see Chapter 15), applicants must notify the local authority where they live about their intention to adopt. The notification must be made at least three months before the adoption order is granted. The local authority must prepare and lodge in court a report about the family, the child and all the circumstances of the case. This is often referred to as a "s.22 Report". There are detailed court rules about what the report should cover. The provisions about "protected children" (formerly ss.32–37 of the 1978 Act) were repealed by the 1995 Act.

1978 Act, s.22; AS 1997, r.2.21(3) and (4); RCS 1994, r.67.21(1); 1995 Act, Schedule 2 para 21

13.18

In some step-parent or relative adoptions, the child has come from overseas and there may be some international aspects to the adoption, such as the need to obtain written consent from a birth parent who resides abroad. These adoptions are not intercountry ones and the adopters do not have to have been assessed under the intercountry adoption rules (see Chapter 15). Similarly, when a child is brought into the UK from overseas by people who have been living and working abroad, and who then wish to adopt the child, that is not an intercountry adoption. Court rules have provisions about having agreements signed abroad when this is necessary.

AS 1997, r.2.23(2); RCS 1994, r.67.5(3)(b)

Pre-court procedures – agency adoptions

13.19

Where a local authority agency wishes to place a child for adoption, with or without a freeing application, there are complicated regulations about procedures and timescales. The adoption agency's crucial stages are the agency adoption panel and the agency decision-maker. No child may be placed by an agency unless its adoption panel has considered the plans for that child and made a recommendation that adoption, with or without freeing, is the best plan for the child. In every case, disputed or undisputed, the agency then has timescales within which it must make a formal decision and notify this to birth parents and others. If the birth parent indicates within a certain time that he or she is in agreement with the plan for adoption and/or freeing, the agency can go ahead without further timescales. If, however, the parent refuses to agree, or does not return the notification within a set time, the agency is tied by strict timescales. It must lodge a freeing order or ensure that an adoption application is lodged by adoptive parents within very short timescales.

Ad Ag Regs 1996, regs.11, 12, 14, 15 and 17

13.20

There are additional requirements on local authority agencies where a child whom they wish to free or have adopted is subject to a supervision requirement. When a child is subject to a supervision requirement and permanence plans are made by the local authority agency, the child must be referred to a hearing for review and consideration of the plans. Where the parent does not agree, and/or the hearing members disagree with the plans, there are detailed timescales which apply.

1995 Act, s.73(4)(c); and Ad Ag Regs 1996, regs.13 and 18

13.21

In all agency adoptions, the placing agency (and this includes English, Welsh and Northern Irish agencies when a child is placed from outwith

Scotland) must prepare and lodge a report for the court. This is often referred to as a "s.23 Report". There are detailed court rules about what the report should cover and these are virtually the same as for "s.22 Reports".

1978 Act, s.23 and s. 65(1); AS 1997, r.2.21(3) and (4); and RCS 1994, r.67.21(1)

Court procedures

13.22

The procedures for adoption and freeing are very similar. Where the child resides in Scotland at the time an application is made for either type of case, it may be heard in the Court of Session or in the local sheriff court. The decision about where to apply is made by the adopter or the authority making the application. Most cases are dealt with in the sheriff court. If the child resides outwith Great Britain at the time the application is made, it can only be heard in the Court of Session.

1978 Act, s.56(2) and (3)

13.23

Forms are provided in the rules of court for adoption and freeing petitions. They are completed and lodged in court. In freeing cases, the local authority agency must lodge a report with every sheriff court application; and in the Court of Session it may either put the information in the petition itself or attach a report. In adoption cases, the s. 22 or s. 23 report (see paragraphs 13.18 and 13.22) is normally lodged at the same time as the application in both courts.

AS 1997, r.2.5(2)(b), r.2.21(2) and Schedule 1 for Forms; RCS 1994, r.67.9, r.67.21 and r.67.22 and Appendix for forms

13.24

In almost all cases, the court will appoint a reporting officer. The reporting officer is required to obtain the agreement of the birth parents, or, if they are not consenting, to confirm that to the court. In sheriff court cases, the reporting officer should report back to the court within 28 days. In Court of Session cases, the reporting officer also seeks the consent of any child who is aged 12 or over – see paragraph 13.26 below.

AS 1997, r.2.7 and r.2.25; r.2.8(1) and r.2.26(1); RCS 1994, r.67.10 and r.67.23; r.67.11(1) and (3) and r.67.24(1) and (3)

13.25

In all sheriff court cases and in almost all Court of Session cases, the court also appoints a curator who must report within 28 days in sheriff court cases. The curator is often the same person as the reporting officer, but not always. The curator is an independent person providing a view of the case from the perspective of the child's welfare. He or she must also give the child's views to the court, provided the child wishes to give them to the curator.

AS 1997, r.2.7 and r.2.25; r.2.8(2) and (3) and r.2.26(2) and (3); RCS 1994, r.67.10 and r.67.23; r.67.11(2) and (4) and r.67.24(2) and (4)

13.26

In Scotland the consent of a child of 12 or over is needed for his or her freeing and/or adoption. The curator seeks this consent in sheriff court cases, and the reporting officer does so in Court of Session cases. The only reason for dispensing with such consent would be if a child was incapable of consenting.

1978 Act, s.12(8) and s.18(8); AS 1997, r.2.8(2) and r.2.26(2); RCS 1994 67.11(1) and 67.24(1)

13.27

Where a child has already been freed for adoption, the question of parental agreement has already been dealt with. A reporting officer should not be appointed, except in a Court of Session adoption where the child is 12 or over, when it is the reporting officer who seeks the child's consent. In all other cases, there is no need for an appointment because no parental agreement is required.

AS 1997 r.2.25(2) – note there is an error in the Rules; RCS 67.23(1)(b)

13.28

After the curator's and reporting officer's reports are received, the court will fix a hearing, although it is not obliged to do so in sheriff court post-freeing adoptions. Where there is a dispute about the adoption or freeing, there will be a proof hearing where evidence will be led. In disputed freeings and adoptions, the court must impose a timetable within which the whole case should be disposed of. Practice Notes for each sheriffdom give further directions about procedures to be followed in sheriff courts.

1978 Act, s.25A; AS 1997 r.2.4, r.2.11 and r.2.28; RCS 1994, r.67.4A, r.67.13 and r.67.25

13.29

Where the birth parent does not agree with the application, the court is asked to dispense with the agreement. The grounds for this are that the parent:
- is not known, cannot be found or is incapable of giving agreement; or
- is withholding agreement unreasonably; or
- has persistently failed without reasonable cause **either** to safeguard and promote the child's health, development and welfare **or** to maintain personal relations and direct contact with the child if he or she is not living with him or her; or
- has seriously ill-treated the child, who is not likely to be reintegrated into the same household.

1978 Act, s.16(1)(b) and (2)

13.30

As indicated in Chapter 12, these grounds are the same as those used in PRO applications. It must be remembered, however, that there are differences between PRO and adoption or freeing processes, and the effects on the child and the birth parents are very different.

13.31

Where parental agreement is not given, the court considers evidence in order to decide whether to dispense with it on one of the grounds listed in paragraph 13.29. If the court is satisfied evidentially, it still has to decide on the basis of the child's welfare and other principles whether to dispense with the agreement; and then whether to grant the freeing or adoption.

13.32

When considering whether to dispense with agreement in a freeing application, the court must also be satisfied that the child has been or is likely to be placed. A freeing order can be sought for a child who is already placed. A child can be placed while a freeing application is going through court.

1978 Act, s.18(3)

13.33

Where a court grants a freeing or adoption order and the child is subject to a supervision requirement, the court may terminate the requirement.

1978 Act, s.12(9) and s.18(9)

Effects of a freeing order

13.34

If a child is freed for adoption, the local authority take **all** parental responsibilities and rights, and the birth parent has nothing left. The child is **not** a "looked after" child, but the local authority are expected to provide at least the same level of service and have the same degree of responsibility as if the child is "looked after". Not all "looked after" duties (e.g. maintenance of contact) are appropriate for children who have been freed. Once a child has been freed, the birth parent has no right to use s.11 of the 1995 Act to seek any parental responsibilities and rights over the child.

1978 Act, s.18(5); and 1995 Act, s.11(3) and (4)

Effects of an adoption order

13.35

When an adoption order is granted in favour of an individual or a couple, that person or those persons hold all the parental responsibilities and rights over the child as if the child had been born to them. Again, the birth parents, if they have not previously lost all rights through a freeing process, now lose all rights to their child and cannot use s.11 of the 1995 Act to get any further court orders. It is possible to have a contact condition attached to an adoption order, but this is not very common and will normally only happen in 'exceptional circumstances'.

1978 s.12; and 1995 Act, s.11(3) and (4)

Adoption support

13.36

Local authority adoption agencies have duties to provide counselling and assistance to adopted children and to adopters, after placement and after adoption. They also have a duty to provide counselling to others affected by adoption, including birth relatives. These duties are wide and apply to the local authority area where the person seeking a service lives, wherever the adoption took place. In addition, they apply to all adoptions, agency and non-agency ones. When a birth parent wants help about adoption, such as advice about tracing a child, he or she is entitled to a service from the local authority in whose area he or she currently lives. The adoption support provisions in the 2002 Act do not apply.

1978 Act, s.1(1) and (2)

Access to birth records

13.37

In Scotland, when an adopted person reaches 16, he or she has automatic rights of access to:
- his or her original birth certificate; and
- his or her court process from the adoption action, and any sheriff court freeing as well.

Counselling services are available but optional. If the adoption was an agency one, the adopted person also has the right to ask the agency which placed him or her to disclose his or her agency records. The agency has discretion whether or not to disclose information to the adopted person, with or without counselling, but most agencies release all or almost all their records to the adopted person.

1978 Act, s.45(5), (6), (6A), (6B) and (7); AS 1997, r.2.14(2)(a) and r.2.33(2)(a); RCS 1994, r.67.32(2)(a); Ad Ag Regs 1996, r.25

13.38

There is no right of access to information for birth parents, but there is an entitlement to support, including counselling, from their local authority agencies. Other people who 'have problems relating to adoption', including members of birth families, are also entitled to counselling. This duty clearly covers providing help to birth families about ways of tracing family members who have been adopted (see paragraph 13.36).

1978 Act, s.1(1)(b) and (2)(c)

13.39

Adoption agencies have discretion to provide access to their records as part of their functions as agencies. For example, they may do so to or for adopted persons under the age of 16 or to others. Subject access to all adoption agency records is exempt by regulations from the DPA 1998, so that subject access is governed by the Ad Ag Regs 1996.

Ad Ag Regs 1996, r.24

14 The Adoption and Children Act 2002

This gives a brief outline of the 2002 Act insofar as it affects Scotland. It is not a full discussion of the Act, most of which does not apply in Scotland.

Introduction

14.1

The 2002 Act is a complete reform of adoption law in England and Wales. It repeals the Adoption Act 1976 when it comes fully into force on 30 December 2005. In addition, some of the Act's sections are important amendments to the 1989 Act. However, some provisions do apply to adoption law in Scotland and Northern Ireland. Section 149 of the 2002 Act lists what applies where. The provisions which clearly amend the 1978 Act, including ss.132–134, and Schedule 3 paragraphs 21–35, are not specifically listed in s.149 but also apply in Scotland.

Provisions applying to Scotland

14.2

In summary, the 2002 Act has five main types of provision which apply to Scotland, although there are other miscellaneous amendments.
1. Provisions restricting the advertising of children, including internet advertising, ss.123 and 124.
2. Provisions ensuring that there is cross-border recognition in Scotland of English and Welsh orders made under the 2002 Act, including adoption and placement orders, Schedule 3, particularly paragraphs 23, 30 and 33.
3. Provisions ensuring that there is continued cross-border recognition in England and Wales of Scottish orders, including freeing, s. 105.
4. New intercountry provision, ss.133 and 134. There are other intercountry provisions which only apply to England and Wales.

5. Provisions allowing Scotland to join the National Adoption Register in the future, if and when that is arranged, ss.125–131.

14.3

The Scottish Executive is responsible for the Commencement Order for implementation. The cross-border recognition and advertising provisions should be in force from 30 December 2005, but not necessarily the others. The intercountry provisions will probably be restated in and implemented as part of the planned reform of adoption law in Scotland (see Chapter 13, paragraph 13.1).

14.4

Scotland will not join the Adoption Register on 30 December 2005. There are provisions in the 2002 Act to allow Scotland to join in the future but it is not known when these will come into force. At present, the Register is operating on a non-statutory basis in England and Wales and there are no plans to implement the statutory provisions in the 2002 Act.

14.5

There will also be new sheriff court and Court of Session rules for cases where children are placed in Scotland under the 2002 Act, by agreement or on placement orders. Their birth parents have the right to ask the court for leave to apply to be heard in the adoption, although leave can only be granted if there has been a change of circumstances. These provisions are in s. 16 of the 1978 Act as amended by Schedule 3, paragraph 23 of the 2003 Act.

Main provisions for England and Wales

14.6

1. From 1 December 2003 unmarried fathers named on birth certificates of children born after then have full parental responsibility by amendment of s. 4 of the 1989 Act (s.111).

2. Since 2003, adoption support services have been established and are being developed further. These include a right to assessment of the need for adoption support (s.4), establishment of adoption support agencies (s.8) and specific provisions giving birth parents rights to seek support after adoption and in tracing (s.3 and s.4). But birth parents do not have a right to trace. There are a considerable number of regulations about adoption support services, and there are separate ones for England and for Wales.

3. Since 2004, there has been an Independent Review Mechanism for prospective adopters who have been refused approval, s.12.

4. Freeing is abolished and placement orders are introduced, ss.18 to 29.

5. Special guardianship orders are introduced, by insertion of new sections, ss.14A–14G, into the 1989 Act (s.115).

6. Step-parent agreements are introduced, by insertion of a new section, s. 4A into the 1989 Act (s.112).

7. There are changes to the grounds for dispensing with parental consent, s.47.

8. Unmarried couples, including same-sex couples, are allowed to adopt together, s.50 and s.144(4) to (6).

Provisions 4–8, like the bulk of the 2002 Act, are in force from 30 December 2005.

14.7

There are also a lot of detailed changes to adoption law for England and Wales, some of which are the same as changes made to Scots law by the 1995 Act amendments to the 1978 Act. These include making the welfare of children the paramount consideration throughout their lives; introducing other principles including taking account of children's views and their religious persuasion, racial origin and cultural and linguistic background; allowing adoption by people who have been resident in the UK for at least a year, instead of having domicile as the only test; and allowing step-parents to adopt on their own without the birth parents having to adopt.

2002 Act, s.1, s.49 and s.50

Consequences for Scotland

14.8

The provisions listed in paragraph 14.6 do not and will not apply directly in Scotland but will have consequences for Scots law and practice. In particular, legal rights given and orders made under the Act will affect people who then move to Scotland. The position of unmarried fathers needs to be checked carefully in every case; and there will be step-parents who have acquired parental responsibility by agreements. There will also be many practical issues arising from the adoption support system (see paragraphs 14.9–14.12 below).

Adoption support

14.9

Adoption support expectations across the borders are affecting and will affect the expectations of adopters, birth families and agencies in Scotland. Where children are placed in Scotland by English and Welsh agencies, and in England and Wales by Scottish agencies, all parties need to be clear about what rights, if any, the parties have to support services under the 2002 Act. Scottish agencies need to be aware that the detailed regulations and guidance for adoption support in England are different from those applying in Wales.

14.10

There are rights in Scotland to adoption support for children, adoptees, adopters and birth families (see Chapter 13, paragraphs 13.36 and 13.38). These are likely to change if there is new adoption legislation in due course (see Chapter 13, paragraph 13.1). However, the adoption support system and duties under the 2002 Act **do not apply** to Scottish agencies.

14.11

This means that when a child is placed by an English or Welsh agency in Scotland, the placing agency must be clear that the local Scottish agency where the child is to live will have no responsibility to provide adoption support under the 2002 Act, only under the 1978 Act. The best practice is for the agencies to negotiate what support is to be provided and by whom.

14.12

This also means that when a child is placed by a Scottish agency in England and Wales, the placing agency must be clear that the local agency and/or the adopters may expect that there will be an adoption support package under the 2002 Act. The Scottish agency will not have such a package because it is not covered by the 2002 Act. Again, good practice is for agencies to negotiate.

15 Intercountry adoption

This chapter deals briefly with some aspects of intercountry adoption.

What is intercountry adoption?

15.1

Although the practice and policy about intercountry adoption are the same throughout the UK, there are a number of detailed differences between the system in Scotland and that for England and Wales. As a result, not all legal details given out on a UK basis will actually be correct for Scotland.

15.2

Intercountry adoption is the term used by professionals, adoption agencies, central government and those who adopt children from outwith the UK. It refers to adoption where:
- the adopter(s) reside in the UK; **and**
- the child resides in a country outside the UK (the state of origin); **and**
- the adopter(s) **either:**
  - bring the child into the UK for the purposes of adoption; **or**
  - adopt the child in his or her state of origin, **and** that order is recognised as adoption in UK law.

15.3

Other adoptions have international aspects: e.g. adoption of a step-child from overseas now living in the UK; or where adopters have returned to live in the UK after working abroad, where they adopted a child but that adoption is not recognised here. However, these are not intercountry adoptions.

Background

15.4

Intercountry adoption in the UK was the subject of good practice procedures for some years but the system had no statutory basis. During the 1990s, there were increasing concerns about abuses and the UK had to legislate to enable it to ratify the 1993 Hague Convention on Protection of Children and Co-operation in Respect of Intercountry Adoption (the Convention).

15.5

The 1999 Act was passed to provide a regulatory system for intercountry adoptions from the three groups of countries listed below. There are differences in the rules for each of the three groups of cases, although the underlying assessment processes are the same. In Scotland, the 1999 Act amends and adds to the 1978 Act for intercountry purposes and provides for regulations and court rules to be made for these adoptions. The regulations, court rules and commencement orders for Scotland are different from those for England and Wales.

Types of countries from which children are adopted

15.6

There are three different types of countries from which intercountry adoptions are arranged. This depends on the state of origin of the child being adopted. And the type of country affects whether there has to be an adoption application in the UK after the child comes here. The three are adoptions from:

- **Convention countries:** countries which have implemented the Convention. In some cases, the child will be adopted in the state of origin, in others adoption will be in the UK.
- **Designated list countries:** countries on the designated list, whose adoption orders are recognised in the UK. There is no need for an adoption application here.
- **Non-Convention/non-designated countries:** countries which are

neither Convention nor designated list ones. After the child enters the UK, it is necessary to apply to adopt here.

15.7

The Department for Education and Skills (DfES) intercountry adoption website (see further reading) lists Convention and designated countries under *Frequently Asked Questions.*

Intercountry adoption processes – pre-court

15.8

In adoption from all three types of countries, prospective adopters must have a home study prepared and be assessed as intercountry adopters by an adoption agency, either a local authority or a voluntary agency. Local authorities must provide an intercountry service. The assessment cannot be done by an independent social worker. The home study is for adoption from a specific country. After assessment, the agency takes the prospective adopters to its adoption panel, then the agency decision-maker approves them as intercountry adopters for the specific country; or does not approve them. When there is approval, the papers are sent by the agency to the Scottish Executive.

1978 Act, s. 1

15.9

If the proposed adoption is from a Convention country, the Scottish Executive is the Central Authority. It processes the papers and if it is agreed that an application can go ahead, the papers are passed to the Home Office for immigration clearance. Once this is completed, the Scottish Executive as Central Authority passes the papers to the central authority for the state of origin and the prospective adopters can make arrangements there.

15.10

If the proposed adoption is from a designated or non-Convention/non-designated country, the process is the same, except the Central Authority is the DfES in London. So the papers go from the Scottish Executive to the DfES and then on to the Home Office.

15.11

After completion of the arrangements in the state of origin, the adopters bring the child into the UK. If the adopters have not gone through the above processes, then they may be guilty of an offence under s. 50A of the 1978 Act, inserted by s. 14 of the 1999 Act. There are four possible situations on return to the UK. The child will have been:

- adopted in a Convention country;
- brought in from a Convention country for adoption here;
- adopted in a designated list country;
- brought in from a non-Convention/non-designated country for adoption here.

1978 Act, s.50A

Intercountry adoption processes – court

15.12

In the first or third situations, there is no court application here, as both types of adoption are recognised in UK law. In the second or fourth situations, there has to be an adoption application here. It is also necessary in these two situations for the adopters to contact their local authority to advise that the child is living with them and give notice of:

- a private fostering arrangement under the 1984 Act; **and**
- their intention to adopt, under s. 22 of the 1978 Act.

1984 Act; 1978 Act, s.22

15.13

If the child has been brought in for adoption from a Convention country, a Convention adoption application is made under s. 17 of the 1978 Act, as amended by s.3 of the 1999 Act. This can be in the sheriff court or the Court of Session. The RCS 1994 and the AS 1997 have been amended to include Convention adoption rules (see paragraph 15.25 below).

1978 Act, s.17; RCS 1994; AS 1997

15.14

If the child has been brought in for adoption from a non-Convention/ non-designated country, the case is similar to a domestic application, under the 1978 Act and the normal court rules.

1978 Act, s.12; RCS 1994; AS 1997

Secondary Legislation

15.15

These are the detailed regulations and court rules which apply.
- Adoption of Children from Overseas (Scotland) Regulations 2001, SSI 2001/236. These cover all intercountry adoptions which are not from Convention countries.
- Intercountry Adoption (Hague Convention) (Scotland) Regulations 2003, SSI 2003/19. These are detailed regulations for Convention adoptions only.
- Act of Sederunt (Child Care and Maintenance Rules) Amendment (1993 Hague Convention Adoption) 2003, SSI 2003/44. These are amendments to the AS 1997 for Convention adoptions only.
- Act of Sederunt (Rules of the Court of Session Amendments) (Miscellaneous) 2004, SSI 2004/52. These include amendments to the RCS 1994 for Convention adoptions only.

The court rules are incorporated into the text of the AS 1997 and RCS 1984 respectively.

Relatives and intercountry adoption

15.16

At present in Scotland, not all the rules described apply to all relatives who want to undertake an intercountry adoption of a child. If the proposed adoption is from a designated or a non-Convention/non-designated country, someone in Scotland wanting to adopt a relative child from abroad does **not** have to have a home study assessment, if the adopter is a relative within the definition in the 1978 Act. Basically, this means a close relative. Sometimes the country of origin of the child insists on one, as Thailand does, and then it will have to be prepared and processed. A close relative will not commit an offence in Scotland if she or he brings a child into the country without having had a home study. **But**, if the adoption is from a Convention country, all the same rules apply to a relative adopter as to a stranger adopter.

15.17

This is in marked contrast to England and Wales, where all adopters in all types of intercountry adoption must have a home study done in advance and will otherwise commit an offence. The Adoption (Bringing Children into the UK) Regulations 2003, SI 2003/1173 make this clear **but do not apply in Scotland.**

Residence period required before adoption can be granted in Scotland

15.18

There are rules about how long a child must live with adopters before an order can be granted (not applied for). These are in s. 13 of the 1978 Act. This has now been amended by the 1999 Act. The periods for intercountry adoptions are:

- six months' residence for all Convention adoptions including relative ones;

- six months' residence for all other relative intercountry adoptions;
- 12 months for all other intercountry adoptions.

Again, the rules are different in England and Wales.

1978 Act, s.13

Entry clearance and acquiring British citizenship for the adoptee

15.19

The immigration rules are extremely complex and specialist immigration advice may be needed. The Home Office Immigration and Nationality Directorate section (IND) has a leaflet, available on the web, about intercountry adoption. All intercountry adopters, including relative ones, should ensure they have entry clearance for the child, in advance of bringing him or her into the UK. There may be difficulties in obtaining entry clearance for bringing in a relative for adoption.

15.20

In stranger intercountry adoptions, the basic rules about citizenship are relatively straightforward, and depend on the type of state of origin and where the adoption took place: i.e. in the UK or abroad.
- Convention adoption abroad confers British citizenship, other than by descent – **BC-OTBD** – provided one adopter is a British citizen and both are "habitually resident" in the UK.
- Convention adoption **and** non-Convention/non-designated adoption in the UK confers BC-OTBD, provided one adopter is a British citizen.
- Designated adoption abroad does not automatically confer BC-OTBD. However, the adopters can apply to register the child as a British citizen under the British Nationality Act 1981, and if successful, BC-OTBD will be conferred.

Registration of foreign adoptions

15.21

The Regis Regs 2003 came into force on 1 June 2003. They allow adopters who have adopted abroad from Convention and designated countries to apply for an entry in the Scottish Adopted Children Register, and the Registrar General to issue an extract from the Register. When a child has been adopted abroad, and the adoption is recognised in the UK, an entry in the Register can be made and an "ordinary" Scottish Extract Birth Certificate will be issued. The Regis Regs 2003 can be used for foreign adoptions which took place before 1 June 2003.

Regis Regs 2003

Glossary

Accommodation
Sections 25 and 26 of the 1995 Act. See Chapter 9.

Adoption agency
Every local authority must have an adoption agency. There are also a number of registered adoption services, which are voluntary agencies registered with the Care Commission, and these are adoption agencies too. See Chapter 13, paragraph 13.7.

Agency adoption
An adoption arranged by an adoption agency.

Care Commission
See Chapter 5.

Child
There is a wide variety of definitions of child. See Chapter 2, paragraph 2.1.

Child assessment order (CAO)
Section 55 of the 1995 Act. See Chapter 8.

Child protection order (CPO)
Sections 57–60 of the 1995 Act. See Chapter 8.

Children "in need"
Sections 22 and 93(4)(a) of the 1995 Act. See Chapter 7.

Contact
This word is used to refer to contact or access between child and parent, child and siblings, etc., whether in the private or public law sector. A contact order, regulating arrangements for contact, is one of the orders listed in s. 11 of the 1995 Act. See Chapter 4.

Day care
Care for children during the day, not overnight. See Chapter 6, paragraphs 6.9 and 6.10, and Chapter 7, paragraph 7.12.

Disabled
Section 23(2) of the 1995 Act in relation to children "in need". See Chapter 7, paragraph 7.9.

Disclosure
See Chapter 2, paragraphs 2.15 and 2.16.

Emergency protection
Section 61 of the 1995 Act. See Chapter 8.

Exclusion order (EO)
Sections 76–80 of the 1995 Act. See Chapter 8.

Freeing
Optional court process by a local authority before adoption, dealing with the agreement of a parent to the adoption. See Chapter 13.

Hearing
A meeting of the children's panel to discuss a child's case. See Chapter 11.

"In need"
See Children "in need".

Intercountry adoption
See Chapter 15.

Interdicts
Court orders prohibiting a person or body from doing something. See Chapter 4, paragraph 4.29.

Local authority
In the 1995 Act, this means the whole local authority. See Chapter 2, paragraph 2.14.

"Looked after" children
Section 17 of the 1995 Act. See Chapter 9.

Principles
The principles in the 1978 and 1995 Acts. See Chapter 2.

Parent
This means different things in different contexts. See Chapter 4 for the private law position and Chapter 13 for the adoption one. In PROs and hearing cases, it is a 'relevant person' who has rights, not a parent. See 'Relevant person'. Genetic parenthood does not always give parental responsibilities and rights: see Chapter 4.

Parental responsibilities and parental rights
Sections 1 and 2 of the 1995 Act. See Chapter 4.

Parental responsibilities order (PRO)
Sections 86–88 of the 1995 Act. See Chapter 12.

Private fostering
A private arrangement between parents and someone who is not a close relative for a period of care for a child. See Chapter 10.

"Relative" adoption
An adoption by a close relative of a child. See Chapter 13.

'Relevant person'
Sections 93(2)(b) and 86 of the 1995 Act. This expression has two different meanings depending on the context:
1. Section 93(2)(b) defines a 'relevant person' for the purpose of the children's hearing system. See Chapter 11, paragraph 11.16.

2. Section 86 defines a 'relevant person' for the purposes of PROs. See Chapter 12, paragraph 12.2.

Residence order
Section 11 of the 1995 Act. The effect of a residence order differs in different circumstances. See Chapter 4.

Respite care
See Chapter 9, paragraph 9.10.

Standards
See Chapter 5, paragraphs 5.5 and 5.6.

Step-parent adoption
An adoption of a child by the spouse of one of his or her birth parents. See Chapter 13.

Further reading and useful websites

Books and publications

Adoption Policy Review Group (APRG), *Adoption: Better Choices for Our Children*, the Report of Phase II, Edinburgh: Scottish Executive, 2005. This is available electronically on the Scottish Executive's website, under Publications, Education, 29 June 2005.

Butterworth's *Scottish Family Law Service*, Edinburgh: Butterworths/ LexisNexis, 1997 onwards. This is a loose-leaf publication, updated every six months.

Green's *Scottish Family Law Legislation and Scottish Social Work Legislation*, Edinburgh: W Green/Thomson, 1997 onwards. These are annotated statutes, etc, published in loose-leaf form and updated regularly.

McNeill P G B, *Adoption of Children in Scotland*, 3rd edition, Edinburgh: W Green/Sweet & Maxwell, 1998.

Norrie K McK, *Children (Scotland) Act 1995 – Annotated version*, 2nd edition, Edinburgh: W Green/Sweet & Maxwell, 2004.

Norrie K McK, *Children's Hearings in Scotland*, Edinburgh: W Green/ Sweet & Maxwell, 1997.

Plumtree A, *Choices for Children,* Edinburgh: Scottish Executive for the Adoption Policy Review Group, Edinburgh, 2003. This is available on the Scottish Executive's website, www.scotland.gov.uk under Publications, Care and Social Work, 11 September 2003.

Scottish Executive, *Supporting Young People Leaving Care in Scotland: Regulations and Guidance on Services for Young People Ceasing to be Looked After by Local Authorities,* Edinburgh: TSO, 2004. This is available on the Scottish Executive's website, www.scotland.gov.uk under Publications, Care and Social Work, 31 March 2004.

Scottish Executive, *Secure and Safe Homes for our Most Vulnerable Children,* Scottish Executive Proposals for Action on the APRG Phase II Report, Edinburgh, 2005. This is available on the Scottish Executive's website, www.scotland.gov.uk, under Publications, Care and Social Work, 30 June 2005.

Scottish Office, *Scotland's Children: The Children (Scotland) Act 1995, Regulations and Guidance:*
- Volume 1: *Support and Protection for Children and their Families*
- Volume 2: *Children Looked After by Local Authorities*
- Volume 3: *Adoption and Parental Responsibilities Orders*

All Edinburgh: HMSO, 1997. These are available on the Scottish Executive's website, www.scotland.gov.uk under Publications, Care and Social Work, 12 October 2004.

Thomson J M, *Family Law in Scotland,* 4th edition, Edinburgh: Butterworths, 2004.

Wilkinson A and Norrie K McN, *Parent and Child,* 2nd edition, K McN Norrie, Edinburgh: W Green, 1999.

Useful websites

British Association for Adoption & Fostering, BAAF
www.baaf.org.uk

Care Commission, the Scottish Commission for the Regulation of Care
www.carecommission.com/index.php

DfES Intercountry Adoption Website. The DfES is responsible for adoption in England. The information about countries and adopting from them is helpful, but the legal input should be treated with caution, because many of the provisions are different in Scotland.
www.dfes.gov.uk/adoption/intercountry/

Disclosure Scotland
www.disclosurescotland.co.uk/

Home Office Immigration and Nationality Direcorate,
www.ind.homeoffice-gov.uk/

Information Commissioner for the UK, responsible for monitoring the DPA 1998
www.informationcommissioner.gov.uk/

Intercountry Adoption Centre, formerly the Overseas Adoption Helpline
www.icacentre.org.uk/

Scottish Courts Service
www.scotcourts.gov.uk/

Scottish Executive
www.scotland.gov.uk/Home